LITURGICAL CALENDAR

for the

ORDER OF PREACHERS

2019

Cycle C

Year I

Prepared for the
U.S. Dominican Provinces
and the
Province of St. Joseph the Worker

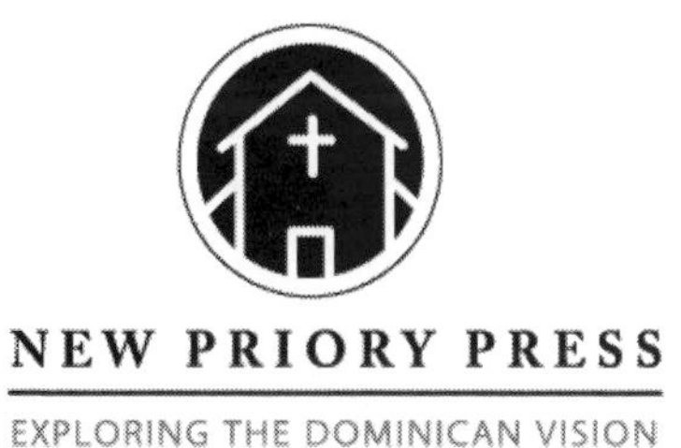

To order more copies of the 2019 Liturgical Calendar, go to
www.newpriorypress.com

For questions and concerns, email us at:
NewPrioryPress@opcentral.org

 Published by New Priory Press, 1910 South Ashland Avenue, Chicago, IL, 60608.

INTRODUCTION

This Liturgical Calendar follows the **Roman Calendar** (1969) adopted by the Order and adapted for use in the Provinces of the United States and the Province of St. Joseph the Worker, by the inclusion of celebrations proper to the Order and celebrations proper to the United States and Nigeria. For the most part, only what pertains to the celebration of the Eucharist is noted.

References to the **Liturgy of the Hours** are limited to indicating the proper week of the four-week psalter to be used and an occasional reference to customs proper to the Order.

I. THE CALENDAR:

A. **Holy Days of Obligation** [USA]: By a decision of the USCCB confirmed by the Congregation for Bishops on July 4, 1992, whenever January 1, the Solemnity of Mary, the Holy Mother of God, or August 15, the Solemnity of The Assumption of the Blessed Virgin Mary, or November 1, All Saints, falls on a Saturday or on a Monday, the precept to attend Mass is abrogated.

B. **Vigil Masses:** Certain celebrations [e.g., The Nativity of the Lord (Christmas), Pentecost Sunday and The Assumption of the Blessed Virgin Mary] have proper Vigil Masses in addition to the Mass for the day itself. These Vigil Masses are intended to be used either before or after First Vespers (Evening Prayer I) of the feastday.

C. **Saturdays in Ordinary Time:** When there is no Obligatory Memorial, an Optional Memorial of the Blessed Virgin Mary is allowed (**RC**, 15). Whenever this Optional Memorial is allowed, the special votive Mass of the Blessed Virgin Mary proper to the Order may be used as an alternative, i.e.:
- OP Votive Mass of the BVM

Wh MASS pref of BVM I or II
RDGS rdgs of the weekday *or* proper:

(A) Eph 1:3-6,16-19 [710.4]/ Resp. Ps [572]/ Lk 1:39-47 [712.5] *or*
(A) Eph 1:3-6,16-19 [710.4]/ Resp. Ps [572]/ Lk 1:39-47 [712.5] *or*
(B) Eph 3:14-19 [740.7]/ Ps 16 [721.1]/ Jn 19:25-27 [712.12]

D. **Celebration of Patronal Feasts:** In addition to the celebrations proper to each province, a community should celebrate the following:

a. Solemnity of the anniversary of the Dedication of their particular church on the anniversary day of the dedication, if the church was consecrated. If the day of dedication is unknown, this solemnity is observed on Oct 22;
b. Solemnity of the titular saint of their church;
c. Solemnity of the principal patron of their house;
d. Feast of the anniversary of the Dedication of the Cathedral;
e. Feast of the principal patron of the diocese, territory, province, or more extensive territory; and
f. Obligatory Memorial of a Saint or Blessed (mentioned in the **Martyrology** or its Appendix) whose body is preserved in their church or oratory.

NB: The celebration of the patron of a province of a religious order is observed as a Feast (**RC** - Table of Liturgical Days, 8d).

E. **The Celebration of Dominican Feastdays:** When the feast of a Dominican Saint or Blessed found in this Calendar is celebrated with the higher rank of a Solemnity, the proper readings given in this Calendar should be arranged as follows:

- lst Reading = Old Testament
  (except during the Easter Season when the first reading is always taken from the New Testament)
- Responsorial Psalm
- 2nd Reading = New Testament
- Gospel Acclamation
- Gospel

When it is a question of celebrating a patronal feast (as listed above), the same principle applies when arranging the readings. When proper readings are not provided, they are taken from the appropriate Common.

On Solemnities the *Gloria* and Creed are said (on Feasts only the *Gloria*) as well as the proper preface, if there is one, or a preface from the appropriate Common is used.

On Memorials the common prefaces for the various categories of Saints may also be used.

II. THE READINGS:

A. The cycles of readings for 2019 are:

Sundays: Year C
Weekdays: Year I

B. In this Liturgical Calendar the references to the daily Mass readings follow the chapter and verse enumeration of the **New American Bible** as revised for the **Lectionary for Mass, 4 vols. (1998-2002)**. The number for the readings given in brackets refers to this same **Lectionary**.

For Sundays, Solemnities and Feasts, the exact text references are given. For Obligatory Memorials and Optional Memorials only the references to the semi-continuous readings are given except for the few Memorials that have assigned readings (e.g., Jan 26 - SS. Timothy and Titus). On days when a Memorial of a saint is celebrated, for compelling pastoral reasons texts may be taken from the Proper of Saints or selected from Commons of the Saints. However, the celebrant will make sure not to omit too often or without sufficient cause the readings assigned for each day in the weekday **Lectionary**. (See: **IL**, n.83).

C. **Choice of Readings for Dominican Celebrations:**

The use of proper readings for Dominican celebrations depends upon the rank of the celebration and is governed by the following norms:

- SOLEMNITY:
  Three readings are used and are taken from the proper.

- FEAST:

  Two readings are used and are taken from the proper or, if there are no proper readings, from the appropriate Common.

- OBLIGATORY OR OPTIONAL MEMORIAL:

  Two readings are used. These may be taken from the proper readings, if there are any, or from the weekday.

III. TYPOGRAPHY OF THIS CALENDAR:

Italics: 1. indicate an element of the liturgy of the day which is optional, e.g., *seq*;
2. indicate an Optional Memorial, e.g., Dec 4, *St. John Damascene*.

A text set off by a short single line indicates explanatory material, e.g.:

----

* = explanatory texts from the Roman rites and documents, e.g., Dec 3;

or

OP = explanatory material taken from Dominican liturgical books, e.g., Dec 22.

The rank of a feastday is indicated by both letters (S, F, M) and typography, e.g.:

- CHRISTMAS (S) **- St. Andrew (F)** - St. Francis Xavier (M)

- Optional Memorials are indicated by *italic type* placed within brackets.

NB: The *Gloria* [gl] and Creed [cr] are said only when indicated in the Liturgical Calendar. The *Gloria* is not said on memorials or weekdays. Days on which Eucharistic Prayer I would have proper *communicantes* are indicated as follows: *prop Roman Canon inserts*.

NB: - Feastdays of whatever rank that are proper only to the United States are indicated by the addition: USA

- Feastdays of whatever rank that are proper only to Nigeria are indicated by the addition: Nigeria

V. LITURGY OF THE HOURS:

In this Calendar, only a reference to the appropriate week of the Four-Week Psalter is provided and this is placed on each Sunday. Solemnities, feasts and certain other days may have proper psalms which replace those of the weekday, however, this is not noted in this Calendar.

VI. ABBREVIATIONS USED IN THIS CALENDAR:

Adv = Advent
Ascen = Ascension
CP = Central Province
cr = Creed
EA = Vicariate of Eastern Africa (Eastern Province)
EP = Evening Prayer
Epiph = Epiphany
GILH = **General Instruction of the Liturgy of the Hours** (1971)
GIRM = **General Instruction of the Roman Missal** (2010)
gl = Gloria
Gr = Green
IL = **Introduction to the Lectionary** (1981)
JW = Province of St. Joseph the Worker
LFM = **Lectionary for Mass** 4 vols. (1998-2002)
MP = Morning Prayer
OHS = **Ordo Hebdomadae Sanctae OP** (1965)
opt mem = Optional Memorial
pref = preface
prop = proper
RC = **Roman Calendar** (1969)
RCIA = **Rite of Christian Initiation of Adults** (1972)
Rd = red
rdgs = readings
Ro = rose
seq = sequence
SP = Southern Province
Vi = violet
Wh = white
WP = Western Province

VII. NECROLOGY:

A combined Necrology of the four Dominican Provinces of Friars in the United States and of the Province of St. Joseph the Worker is appended to this Liturgical Calendar, by date (p.57 ff) and by name (p. 111).

DECEMBER 2018

2 Sun - **1st SUNDAY OF ADVENT** HOURS Week I

Vi MASS cr, pref I of Adv

RDGS [3] Jer 33:14-16/ 1 Thes 3:12–4:2/ Lk 21:25-28,34-36

----

* Begin Cycle C for Sunday rdgs and Year I for weekday rdgs.
* Mass pref until Dec 16 inclusive is pref I of Adv, i.e., for Sundays, weekdays and feasts which have no prop pref.

----

3 Mon - St. Francis Xavier, Priest (M)

Wh MASS pref I of Adv

RDGS [175] Is 2:1-5 (1st choice)/ Mt 8:5-11

4 Tue - Advent Weekday

Vi MASS pref I of Adv

RDGS [176] Is 11:1-10/ Lk 10:21-24

[*Wh - St. John Damascene, Priest and Doctor of the Church*]

5 Wed - Advent Weekday

Vi MASS pref I of Adv

RDGS [177] Is 25:6-10a/ Mt 15:29-37

6 Thu -Advent Weekday

Vi MASS pref I of Adv

RDGS [178] Is 26:1-6/ Mt 7:21,24-27

[*Wh - St. Nicholas, Bishop*]

7 Fri - St. Ambrose, Bishop and Doctor of the Church (M)

Wh MASS pref I of Adv

RDGS [179] Is 29:17-24/ Mt 9:27-31

----

* EP = First Vespers (Evening Prayer I) of The Immaculate Conception of the BVM.

----

8 Sat - **THE IMMACULATE CONCEPTION OF THE BLESSED VIRGIN MARY** (Patronal Feastday of the United States of America)

Today is a holy day of obligation in the USA.

Wh MASS gl, cr, prop pref

RDGS [689] Gn 3:9-15,20/ Eph 1:3-6,11-12/ Lk 1:26-38

----

* EP = First Vespers (Evening Prayer I) of the 1st Sunday of Advent.

=============

9 Sun - **2nd SUNDAY OF ADVENT** HOURS Week II

Vi MASS cr, pref I of Adv

RDGS [6] Bar 5:1-9/ Phil 1:4-6,8-11/ Lk 3:1-6

December

10 Mon - Advent Weekday
Vi MASS pref I of Adv
RDGS [181] Is 35:1-10/ Lk 5:17-26
11 Tue - Advent Weekday
Vi MASS pref I of Adv
RDGS [182] Is 40:1-11 / Mt 18:12-14
[*Wh - St. Damasus I, Pope*]
12 Wed - **Our Lady of Guadalupe (F)** [USA]
Wh MASS gl, pref I or II of BVM
RDGS [690A] Zec 2:14-17 or Rv 11:19a; 12:1-6a, 10ab/ Lk 1:26-38 or Lk 1:39-47 or any rdgs from the Common of the BVM [707-712]

JW For the Province of St. Joseph the Worker:
12 - Advent Weekday
Vi MASS pref I or Adv
RDGS [183] Is 40:25-31/ Mt 11:28-30

----

13 Thu - St. Lucy, Virgin and Martyr (M)
Rd MASS pref I of Adv
RDGS [184] Is 41:13-20/ Mt 11:11-15
14 Fri - St. John of the Cross, Priest and Doctor of the Church (M)
Wh MASS pref I of Adv
RDGS [185] Is 48:17-19/ Mt 11:16-19
15 Sat - Advent Weekday
Vi MASS pref I of Adv
RDGS [186] Sir 48:1-4,9-11/ Mt 17:9a,10-13

==============

16 Sun - **3rd SUNDAY OF ADVENT** HOURS Week III
Vi/Ro MASS cr, pref I of Adv
RDGS [9] Zep 3:14-18a/ Phil 4:4-7/ Lk 3:10-18
17 Mon - **Advent Weekday**
Vi MASS pref II of Adv
RDGS [193] Gn 49:2,8-10/ Mt 1:1-17

----

* Mass pref for Dec 17-24 inclusive is pref II of Adv.

----

18 Tue - **Advent Weekday**
Vi MASS pref II of Adv
RDGS [194] Jer 23:5-8/ Mt 1:18-25

19 Wed - **Advent Weekday**
Vi MASS pref II of Adv
RDGS [195] Jgs 13:2-7,24-25a/ Lk 1:5-25

20 Thu - **Advent Weekday**
Vi MASS pref II of Adv
RDGS [196] Is 7:10-14/ Lk 1:26-38

21 Fri - **Advent Weekday**
Vi MASS pref II of Adv
RDGS [197] Sg 2:8-14 or Zep 3:14-18a/ Lk 1:39-45

[*St. Peter Canisius, Priest and Doctor of the Church*]

----

* During this period of Advent and the Octave of Christmas all memorials are optional. If observed, they are celebrated by using the Collect of the Saint in place of the Collect of the day.

----

22 Sat - **Advent Weekday**
Vi MASS pref II of Adv
RDGS [198] 1 Sm 1:24-28/ Lk 1:46-56

OP On this the anniversary of the approval of our Order (Dec 22, 1216), special prayers for this intention may be made at Mass and Vespers (Evening Prayer).

=============

23 Sun - **4th SUNDAY OF ADVENT** HOURS Week IV
Vi MASS cr, pref II of Adv
RDGS [12] Mi 5:1-4a/ Heb 10:5-10/ Lk 1:39-45

24 Mon - **Advent Weekday**
Vi MASS pref II of Adv
RDGS [200] 2 Sm 7:1-5,8b-12,14a,16/ Lk 1:67-79

----

* Christmas Time begins with First Vespers (Evening Prayer I) of the Nativity.
* The Vigil Mass is used on the evening of December 24, either before or after First Vespers (Evening Prayer I) of the Nativity.

OP Before Mass during the Night on The Nativity of the Lord it is appropriate that the Office of Readings be celebrated as a vigil. (GILH, n.215)

At the conclusion of this celebration, as is the custom in the liturgical tradition of our Order, the Genealogy according to Matthew (1:1-16) may be sung.

If necessary, the chant, that is the solemn proclamation of the Genealogy, may be sung in the manner proper to the Gospel by a cantor who is not a deacon (as the norms for the singing of the Easter Proclamation allow). It may be sung either in Latin using the Gregorian chant in the **Missale et Lectionarium OP** (1985), pp.510-514, or in the vernacular using a suitable melody composed or adapted for it. It may also be proclaimed in a recitative style with a musical harmony as a background and with the addition *ad libitum* of some acclamations for the people interspersed throughout the proclamation.

* EP = First Vespers (Evening Prayer I) of The Nativity of the Lord.

----

25 Tue - **THE NATIVITY OF THE LORD (Christmas) (S)**

Today is a holy day of obligation in the USA.

Wh MASS gl, cr, pref I-III of the Nativity, *prop Roman Canon inserts*
Mass during the Day: *seq*

RDGS Vigil: [13] Is 62:1-5/ Acts 13:16-17,22-25/ Mt 1:1-25 or 1:18-25
Night: [14] Is 9:1-6/ Ti 2:11-14/ Lk 2:1-14
Dawn: [15] Is 62:11-12/ Ti 3:4-7/ Lk 2:15-20
Day: [16] Is 52:7-10/ Heb 1:1-6/ Jn 1:1-18 or 1:1-5,9-14

OP At the Mass during the Day the sequence *Laetabundus* may be used, as found in the **Missale et Lectionarium OP** (1985), pp.503-505.

----

26 Wed - **St. Stephen, The First Martyr (F)**

Rd MASS gl, pref I-III of the Nativity, *prop Roman Canon inserts*
RDGS [696] Acts 6:8-10;7:54-59/ Mt 10:17-22

27 Thu - **St. John, Apostle and Evangelist (F)**

Wh MASS gl, pref I-III of the Nativity, *prop Roman Canon inserts*
RDGS [697] 1 Jn 1:1-4/ Jn 20:1a,2-8

28 Fri - **The Holy Innocents, Martyrs (F)**

Rd MASS gl, pref I-III of the Nativity, *prop Roman Canon inserts*
RDGS [698] 1 Jn 1:5–2:2/ Mt 2:13-18

29 Sat - **Fifth Day within the Octave of The Nativity of the Lord**

Wh MASS gl, pref I-III of the Nativity, *prop Roman Canon inserts*
RDGS [202] 1 Jn 2:3-11/ Lk 2:22-35

[*St. Thomas Becket, Bishop and Martyr*]

----

* EP = First Vespers (Evening Prayer I) of The Holy Family of Jesus, Mary, and Joseph.

=============

30 Sun - **The Holy Family of Jesus, Mary, and Joseph (F)** HOURS Week I
Wh MASS gl, cr, pref I-III of the Nativity, *prop Roman Canon inserts*
RDGS[17] Sir 3:2-7,12-14/ Col 3:12-21 or 3:12-17/ Lk 2:41-52 or, for Year C, 1 Sm 1:20-22,24-28/ 1 Jn 3:1-2,21-24/ Lk 2:41-52

31 Mon - **Seventh Day within the Octave of The Nativity of the Lord**
Wh MASS gl, pref I-III of the Nativity, *prop Roman Canon inserts*
RDGS [204] 1 Jn 2:18-21/ Jn 1:1-18
[*St. Sylvester I, Pope*]

----

* EP = First Vespers (Evening Prayer I) of the Solemnity of Mary, The Holy Mother of God.

JANUARY 2019

1 Tue - **SOLEMNITY OF MARY, THE HOLY MOTHER OF GOD (S)**
THE OCTAVE DAY OF THE NATIVITY OF THE LORD
This Solemnity is a holy day of obligation in the USA.
Wh MASS gl, cr, pref I of BVM, *prop Roman Canon inserts*
RDGS [18] Nm 6:22-27/ Gal 4:4-7/ Lk 2:16-21

2 Wed - SS. Basil the Great and Gregory Nazianzen, Bishops and Doctors of the Church (M)
Wh MASS pref I-III of the Nativity
RDGS [205] 1 Jn 2:22-28/ Jn 1:19-28

3 Thu - Christmas Weekday
Wh MASS pref I-III of the Nativity
RDGS [206] 1 Jn 2:29–3:6/ Jn 1:29-34
[*Wh - The Most Holy Name of Jesus]*
MASS Votive Mass of The Most Holy Name of Jesus
RDGS prop Phil 2:1-11 [136A]/ Ps 8 [753.1]/ Lk 2:21-24 or from the Votive Mass of the Most Holy Name of Jesus - Lectionary, vol. IV, 983-988

WP Titular feast of the Western Province:
- The Most Holy Name of Jesus (F)
Wh MASS gl, Votive Mass of the Most Holy Name of Jesus
RDGS prop as above

----

4 Fri - St. Elizabeth Ann Seton, Religious (M) [USA]
Wh MASS pref I-III of the Nativity
RDGS [207] 1 Jn 3:7-10/ Jn 1:35-42

JW For the Province of St. Joseph the Worker.
4 - St. Zedíslava of Lemberk, OP (M)
Wh MASS pref I-III of the Nativity
RDGS [207] 1 Jn 3:7-10/ Jn 1:35-42
As above, or prop: 1 Jn 3:14-18 [740.16]/ Ps 112 [739.7]/ Mt 16:24-27 [742.6]

NB: In the United States the obligatory memorial of St. Elizabeth Ann Seton takes precedence over that of St. Zedíslava of Lemberk, OP. Some Provinces may observe it on Nov. 28th.

----

5 Sat - St. John Neumann, Bishop (M) [USA]
Wh MASS pref I-III of the Nativity
RDGS [208] 1 Jn 3:11-21/ Jn 1:43-51

JW For the Province of St. Joseph the Worker.
5 - Christmas Weekday
Wh MASS pref I-III of the Nativity
RDGS [208] 1 Jn 3:11-21/ Jn 1:43-51

----

* EP = First Vespers (Evening Prayer I) of The Epiphany of the Lord.

==============

6 Sun - **THE EPIPHANY OF THE LORD (S)** HOURS Week II
Wh MASS gl, cr, pref of Epiph, *prop Roman Canon inserts*
RDGS [20] Is 60:1-6/ Eph 3:2-3a,5-6/ Mt 2:1-12

OP The sequence *Laetabundus* may be used, as found in the **Missale et Lectionarium OP** (1985), pp.503-505.
* Where it is the practice, if appropriate, the moveable Feasts of the current year may be proclaimed after the Gospel, according to the formula in the Roman Missal, pp.1291-1292.

----

7 Mon - St. Raymond of Penyafort, OP, Priest (M)
Wh MASS pref of Epiph or pref I-III of the Nativity
RDGS [212] 1 Jn 3:22–4:6/ Mt 4:12-17,23-25
As above, or, prop: 2 Cor 5:14-21 [722.7] or Ez 33:1,7-11 or Gal 5:16-17,22-23a,24-25 [765.10]/ Ps 103 [739.6] or Ps 119 [450]/ Mt 5:13-19 [730.1] or Lk 12:42-44,48b
8 Tue - Christmas Weekday
Wh MASS pref of Epiph or pref I-III of the Nativity
RDGS [213] 1 Jn 4:7-10/ Mk 6:34-44

9 Wed - Christmas Weekday
Wh MASS pref of Epiph or pref I-III of the Nativity
RDGS [214] 1 Jn 4:11-18/ Mk 6:45-52
[*Wh - St. Adrian of Canterbury, Abbot - Nigeria*]
10 Thu - Christmas Weekday
Wh MASS pref of Epiph, or pref I-III of the Nativity
RDGS [215] 1 Jn 4:19–5:4/ Lk 4:14-22a
11 Fri - Christmas Weekday
Wh MASS pref of Epiph, or pref I-III of the Nativity
RDGS [216] 1 Jn 5:5-13/ Lk 5:12-16
12 Sat - Christmas Weekday
Wh MASS pref of Epiph, or pref I-III of the Nativity
RDGS [217] 1 Jn 5:14-21/ Jn 3:22-30

----

* EP = First Vespers (Evening Prayer I) of The Baptism of the Lord.

=============

13 Sun - **The Baptism of the Lord (F)** HOURS Week I
Wh MASS gl, cr, prop pref
RDGS [21] Is 42:1-4,6-7/ Acts 10:34-38/ Lk 3:15-16,21-22 or, for Year C, Is 40:1-5,9-11/ Ti 2:11-14; 3:4-7/ Lk 3:15-16,21-22

----

* Christmas Time ends with Second Vespers (Evening Prayer II) of The Baptism of the Lord.

----

14 Mon - Weekday (1st Week in Ordinary Time)
Gr RDGS [305] Heb 1:1-6/ Mk 1:14-20
15 Tue - SS. Francis Fernández de Capillas, OP, Priest, Peter Sanz, OP, Bishop, and Companions, Martyrs in China (M)
Rd RDGS [306] Heb 2:5-12/ Mk 1:21-28
As above, or, prop: Wis 3:1-9 [713.5]/ Ps 116 [1013.7]/ Mt 16:24-27 [742.6]
16 Wed - Weekday
Gr RDGS [307] Heb 2:14-18/ Mk 1:29-39
17 Thu - St. Anthony, Abbot (M)
Wh RDGS [308] Heb 3:7-14/ Mk 1:40-45
18 Fri - St. Margaret of Hungary, OP, Virgin (M)
Wh RDGS [309] Heb 4:1-5,11/ Mk 2:1-12
As above, or, prop: Col 3:12-17 [812.11] or Est C:14-23,30 or Rom 12:1-2,9-13 [802.2 - short form]/ Ps 27 [813.2]/ Jn 12:24-26 [815.13]

OP For the nuns of the Order:

- St. Margaret of Hungary, OP, Virgin (F)

Wh MASS gl, pref of Virgins and Religious

RDGS prop as above

* The Week of Prayer for Christian Unity begins today.

----

19 Sat - Weekday

Gr RDGS [310] Heb 4:12-16/ Mk 2:13-17

[*Rd - St. Fabian, Pope and Martyr - Nigeria*]

[*Rd - St. Sebastian, Martyr - Nigeria*]

[*Wh - BVM on Sat or OP Votive Mass]*

MASS pref I or II of BVM

RDGS as above or OP Votive Mass

=============

20 Sun - **2nd Sunday in Ordinary Time** HOURS Week II

Gr MASS gl, cr, pref I-VIII of Sundays in Ordinary Time

RDGS [66] Is 62:1-5/ 1 Cor 12:4-11/ Jn 2:1-11

21 Mon - St. Agnes, Virgin and Martyr (M)

Rd RDGS [311] Heb 5:1-10/ Mk 2:18-22

22 Tue - Day of Prayer for the Legal Protection of Unborn Children [USA]

Gr The Liturgy of the Hours follows the weekday.

RDGS[312] Heb 6:10-20/ Mk 2:23-28

Or:

Wh MASS "For Giving Thanks to God for the Gift of Human Life" - *Roman Missal,* For Various Occasions - no.48/1.

RDGS From *Lectionary for Mass Supplement* [947A-947E]

Or:

Vi MASS "For the Presevation of Peace and Justice" - *Roman Missal*, For Various Occasions - no.30

RDGS From *Lectionary for Mass* (vol. IV), "For Peace and Justice" [887-891]

JW For the Province of St. Joseph the Worker

22 - Weekday

Gr RDGS [312] Heb 6:10-20/ Mk 2:23-28

[*Rd - St. Vincent, Deacon and Martyr*]

----

23 Wed - Weekday

Gr RDGS [313] Heb 7:1-3,15-17/ Mk 3:1-6

[*Rd - St. Vincent, Deacon and Martyr - USA*]

[*Wh - St. Marianne Cope, Virgin - USA*]

24 Thu - St. Francis de Sales, Bishop and Doctor of the Church (M)
Wh RDGS [314] Heb 7:25–8:6/ Mk 3:7-12
25 Fri - **The Conversion of St. Paul the Apostle (F)**
Wh MASS gl, pref I of Apostles
RDGS [519] Acts 22:3-16 or Acts 9:1-22/ Mk 16:15-18

---

* The Week of prayer for Christian Unity ends today.

---

26 Sat - SS. Timothy and Titus, Bishops (M)
Wh RDGS [520] 2 Tm 1:1-8 or Ti 1:1-5/ [316] Mk 3:20-21

=============

27 Sun - **3rd Sunday in Ordinary Time** HOURS Week III
Gr MASS gl, cr, pref I-VIII of Sundays in Ordinary Time
RDGS [69] Neh 8:2-4a,5-6,8-10/ 1 Cor 12:12-30 or 12:12-14,27/ Lk 1:1-4; 4:14-21
28 Mon - **St. Thomas Aquinas, OP, Priest and Doctor of the Church (F)**
Wh MASS gl, prop pref
RDGS prop: Wis 7:7-10,15-16 [725.2] or Eph 3:8-12 [728.4]/ Ps 37 [727.2]/ Jn 17:11-19 [718.7] or Jn 16:23b-28 [296] or Mt 5:13-19 [730.1]
29 Tue - Weekday
Gr RDGS [318] Heb 10:1-10/ Mk 3:31-35
30 Wed - Weekday
Gr RDGS [319] Heb 10:11-18/ Mk 4:1-20
31 Thu - St. John Bosco, Priest (M)
Wh RDGS [320] Heb 10:19-25/ Mk 4:1-20

FEBRUARY 2019

1 Fri - Weekday
Gr RDGS [321] Heb 10:32-39/ Mk 4:26-34
2 Sat - **The Presentation of the Lord (F)**
Wh MASS gl, *seq*, prop pref
RDGS [524] Mal 3:1-4/ Heb 2:14-18/ Lk 2:22-40 or 2:22-32

---

* If candles are blessed, the blessing is done before Mass following the rite in the **Missal.**

OP At Mass the sequence *Laetabundus* may be used, as found in the **Missale et Lectionarium OP** (1995), pp.503-505.

=============

February

3 Sun - **4th Sunday in Ordinary Time** HOURS Week IV

Gr MASS gl, cr, pref I-VIII of Sundays in Ordinary Time

RDGS [72] Jer 1:4-5,17-19/ 1 Cor 12:31–13:13 or 13:4-13/ Lk 4:21-30

----

* The blessing of throats may be done following the rite approved for the U.S.A.

----

4 Mon - St. Catherine de' Ricci, OP, Virgin (M)

Wh RDGS [323] Heb 11:32-40/ Mk 5:1-20

As above, or, prop: Rv 19:1,5-9a [732.1] or Rom 8:35,37-39 [112]/ Ps 27 [813.2]/ Mk 8:34–9:1 [339]

5 Tue - St. Agatha, Virgin and Martyr (M)

Rd RDGS [324] Heb 12:1-4/ Mk 5:21-43

6 Wed - St. Paul Miki and Companions, Martyrs (M)

Rd RDGS [325] Heb 12:4-7,11-15/ Mk 6:1-6

7 Thu - Weekday

Gr RDGS [326] Heb 12:18-19,21-24/ Mk 6:7-13

OP Today at the Conventual Mass the Anniversary of Deceased Parents is celebrated.

Wh/Vi/Blk - Anniversary of Deceased Parents

MASS pref I-V for the Dead

RDGS From the Masses for the Dead [1011-1016], especially: Rom 14:7-9,10c-12 [1014.6]/ Ps 122 [1013.8]/ Jn 17:24-26 [1016.18]

* The liturgy of the hours follows the weekday, not the anniversary.

----

8 Fri - Weekday

Gr RDGS [327] Heb 13:1-8/ Mk 6:14-29

[*Wh - St. Jerome Emiliani, Priest*]

[*Wh - St. Josephine Bakhita, Virgin*]

9 Sat - Weekday

Gr RDGS [328] Heb 13:15-17,20-21/ Mk 6:30-34

[*Wh - BVM on Sat or OP Votive Mass*]

MASS pref I or II of BVM

RDGS as above or OP Votive Mass

=============

10 Sun - **5th Sunday in Ordinary Time** HOURS Week I

GR MASS gl, cr, pref I-VIII of Sundays in Ordinary Time

RDGS [75] Is 6:1-2a,3-8/ 1 Cor 15:1-11 or 15:3-8,11/ Lk 5:1-11

11 Mon - Weekday
Gr RDGS [329] Gn 1:1-19/ Mk 6:53-56
[*Wh - Our Lady of Lourdes*]
MASS pref I or II of BVM
12 Tue - Weekday
Gr RDGS [330] Gn 1:20–2:4a/ Mk 7:1-13
[*Wh - Bl. Reginald of Orléans, OP, Priest*]
RDGS As above, or, prop: Phil 4:4-9 [740.10]/ Ps 63 [813.8]/ Mk 6:7-13 [326]
13 Wed - Bl. Jordan of Saxony, OP, Priest (M)
Wh RDGS [331] Gn 24b-9,15-17/ Mk 7:14-23
As above, or, prop: Eph 4:1-7,11-13 [722.8]/ Ps 96 [721.5]/ Lk 10:1-9 [724.8]
14 Thu - SS. Cyril, Monk, and Methodius, Bishop (M)
Wh RDGS [332] Gn 2:18-25/ Mk 7:24-30
15 Fri - Weekday
Gr RDGS [333] Gn 3:1-8/ Mk 7:31-37
16 Sat - Weekday
Gr RDGS [334] Gn 3:9-24/ Mk 8:1-10
[*Wh - BVM on Sat or OP Votive Mass*]
MASS pref I or II of BVM
RDGS as above or OP Votive Mass

=============

17 Sun - **6th Sunday in Ordinary Time** HOURS Week II
Gr MASS gl, cr, pref I-VIII of Sundays in Ordinary Time
RDGS [78] Jer 17:5-8/ 1 Cor 15:12,16-20/ Lk 6:17,20-26
18 Mon - Weekday
Gr RDGS [335] Gn 4:1-15,25/ Mk 8:11-13
[*Wh - Bl. John of Fiesole (Fra Angelico), OP, Priest*]
RDGS As above, or, prop: Rom 8:5-11/ Ps 73:1,23-26,28/ Mt 5:16; 6:19-23; 7:17,20-21
19 Tue - Weekday
GR RDGS [336] Gn 6:5-8; 7:1-5,10/ Mk 8:14-21
20 Wed - Weekday
Gr RDGS [337] Gn 8:6-13,20-22/ Mk 8:22-26
21 Thu - Weekday
Gr RDGS [338] Gn 9:1-13/ Mk 8:27-33
[*Wh - St. Peter Damian, Bishop and Doctor of the Church*]

22 Fri - **The Chair of St. Peter the Apostle (F)**
Wh MASS gl, pref I of Apostles
RDGS [535] 1 Pt 5:1-4/ Mt 16:13-19
23 Sat - St. Polycarp, Bishop and Martyr (M)
Rd RDGS [340] Heb 11:1-7/ Mk 9:2-13
=============

24 Sun - **7th Sunday in Ordinary Time** HOURS Week III
Gr MASS gl, cr, pref I-VIII of Sundays in Ordinary Time
RDGS [81] 1 Sm 26:2,7-9,12-13,22-23/ 1 Cor 15:45-49/ Lk 6:27-38
25 Mon - Weekday
Gr RDGS [341] Sir 1:1-10/ Mk 9:14-29
26 Tue - Weekday
Gr RDGS [342] Sir 2:1-11/ Mk 9:30-37
[*Wh - St. Alexander of Alexandria, Bishop - Nigeria*]
27 Wed - Weekday
Gr RDGS [343] Sir 4:11-19/ Mk 9:38-40
28 Thu - Weekday
Gr RDGS [344] Sir 5:1-8/ Mk 9:41-50

March 2019

1 Fri - Weekday
Gr RDGS [345] Sir 6:5-17/ Mk 10:1-12
2 Sat - Weekday
Gr EDGS [346] Sir 17:1-15/ Mk 10:13-16
[*Wh - BVM on Sat or OP Votive Mass*]
MASS pref I or II of BVM
RDGS as above or OP Votive Mass
=============

3 Sun - **8th Sunday in Ordinary Time** HOURS Week IV
Gr MASS gl, cr, pref I-VIII of Sundays In Ordinary Time
RDGS [84] Sir 27:4-7/ 1 Cor 15:54-58/ Lk 6:39-45
4 Mon - Weekday
Gr RDGS [347] Sir 17:20-24/ Mk 10:17-27
[*Wh - St. Casimir*]
5 Tue - Weekday
Gr RDGS [348] Sir 35:1-12/ Mk 10:28-31

SEASON OF LENT

OP 1. The season of Lent runs from Ash Wednesday until the Evening Mass of the Lord's Supper on Holy Thursday exclusive. This season retains its penitential character and serves as a preparation for the celebration of Easter.

2. Penitential practices during Lent: According to Church law each Friday in Lent is observed as a day of abstinence; Ash Wednesday and Good Friday are observed as days of fast and abstinence.

Keeping in mind the tradition and legislation of the Order, the following should be observed to the extent that they apply: (a) determinations laid down by various Provincial Chapters concerning the forms of fasting and abstinence; (b) the statutes of particular Conventual Chapters; and (c) the Directories for Nuns regarding proper acts of self-denial for their communities.

3. If it seems appropriate, on Ash Wednesday or on other days during Lent in place of the former rite of the penitential psalms some communal penitential celebration or "rite of reconciliation" may be held, whether it be sacramental or non-sacramental (according to the spirit of the **Rite of Penance**, nn.36-37). However, this celebration may not immediately precede Mass.

* During Lent the *Alleluia* is always omitted at Mass and Office. The *Gloria* is said at Mass only on solemnities and feasts.

LITURGY OF THE HOURS

OP Compline (Night Prayer):

1. If Compline (Night Prayer) is sung, the *In pace* response may be used in place of "Into your hands." The antiphons *Evigila* or *O Rex* may be used in place of the Gospel canticle antiphon "Keep us safe."

2. If Compline (Night Prayer) is not sung, the antiphons *Evigila* and *O Rex* may be used for the Gospel canticle at Vespers (Evening Prayer) in place of the regular antiphon. This may be done at First Vespers (Evening Prayer I) and Second Vespers (Evening Prayer II) of Sundays of Lent.

3. The chant *Media vita* may be used in place of the short response whether at Compline (Night Prayer) or at Vespers (Evening Prayer) – or even at other celebrations, such as a penitential liturgy on Ash Wednesday or on Thursday of Holy Week (before the beginning of the Paschal Triduum). Note that this chant is not an antiphon (as wrongly indicated in our books) and should no longer be used as such.

----

6 Wed - **ASH WEDNESDAY** HOURS Week IV

Vi MASS pref III or IV of Lent

RDGS [219] Jl 2:12-18/ 2 Cor 5:20–6:2/ Mt 6:1-6,16-18

----

* Psalms from Week IV of the psalter are used at the Liturgy of the Hours today and for the remainder of this week. The psalms from Friday, Week III, may be used at Morning Prayer today.

* At Mass the penitential rite is omitted.
* The celebrant blesses and distributes ashes after the homily.
* According to a response from the Congregation for Divine Worship (Jan, 1975) other persons may be associated with the Bishop or Priest in the imposition of ashes, e.g., Deacons, Extraordinary Ministers of Holy Communion and other lay persons, when there is true pastoral need.

  Extraordinary Ministers of Holy Communion and Deacons may bring blessed ashes to the sick and those confined to their homes. If a minister is not available, a member of the family or another person may bring the blessed ashes to a shut-in, using one of the formulas in the *Roman Missal* to impose ashes.
* The blessing and distribution of ashes may also take place outside Mass. In this case, the rite is preceded by a Liturgy of the Word, with the Entrance Antiphon, the Collect, and the readings with their chants as at Mass. Then there follow the Homily and the blessing and distribution of ashes. The rite is concluded with the Universal Prayer, the Blessing and the Dismissal of the Faithful.

OP When for pastoral reasons the blessing and distribution of ashes takes place outside Mass, it may be appropriately joined to some hour of the Office, especially Midday Prayer or the Office of Readings.

----

7 Thu - Thursday after Ash Wednesday
Vi MASS pref I-IV of Lent
RDGS [220] Dt 30:15-20/ Lk 9:22-25
[*SS. Perpetua and Felicity, Martyrs*]

----

* During Lent all memorials are optional. If observed, they are celebrated by using the Collect of the Saint in place of the Collect of the day.

----

8 Fri - Friday after Ash Wednesday
Vi MASS pref I-IV of Lent
RDGS [221] Is 58:1-9a/ Mt 9:14-15
[*St. John of God, Religious*]

9 Sat - Saturday after Ash Wednesday
Vi MASS pref I-IV of Lent
RDGS [222] Is 58:9b-14/ Lk 5:27-32
[*St. Frances of Rome, Religious*]

=============

10 Sun - **1st SUNDAY OF LENT** HOURS Week I
Vi MASS cr, prop pref
RDGS [24] Dt 26:4-10/ Rom 10:8-13/ Lk 4:1-13

----

* On this Sunday is celebrated the rite of "election" or "enrollment of names" for the catechumens who are to be admitted to the Sacraments of Christian Initiation at the Easter Vigil, using the proper prayers and intercessions in the **Roman Missal**.

----

11 Mon - Lenten Weekday
Vi MASS pref I-IV of Lent
RDGS [224] Lv 19:1-2,11-18/ Mt 25:31-46

12 Tue - Lenten Weekday
Vi MASS pref I-IV of Lent
RDGS [225] Is 55:10-11/ Mt 6:7-15

13 Wed - Lenten Weekday
Vi MASS pref I-IV of Lent
RDGS [226] Jon 3:1-10/ Lk 11:29-32

14 Thu - Lenten Weekday
Vi MASS pref I-IV of Lent
RDGS [227] Est C:12,14-16,23-25/ Mt 7:7-12

15 Fri - Lenten Weekday
Vi MASS pref I-IV of Lent
RDGS [228] Ez 18:21-28/ Mt 5:20-26

16 Sat - Lenten Weekday
Vi MASS pref I-IV of Lent
RDGS [229] Dt 26:16-19/ Mt 5:43-48

=============

17 Sun - **2nd SUNDAY OF LENT** HOURS Week II
Vi MASS cr, prop pref
RDGS [27] Gn 15:5-12,17-18/ Phil 3:17–4:1 or 3:20–4:1/ Lk 9:28b-36

18 Mon - Lenten Weekday
Vi MASS pref I-IV of Lent
RDGS [230] Dn 9:4b-10/ Lk 6:36-38
[*St. Cyril of Jerusalem, Bishop and Doctor of the church*]

----

* EP = First Vespers (Evening Prayer I) of St. Joseph, Spouse of the Blessed Virgin Mary.

----

19 Tue - **ST JOSEPH, Spouse of the Blessed Virgin Mary (S)**
Wh MASS gl, cr, prop pref
RDGS [543] 2 Sm 7:4-5a,12-14a,16/ Rom 4:13,16-18,22/ Mt 1:16,18-21,24a or Lk 2:41-51a
20 Wed - Lenten Weekday
Vi MASS pref I-IV of Lent
RDGS [232] Jer 18:18-20/ Mt 20:17-28
21 Thu - Lenten Weekday
Vi MASS pref I-IV of Lent
RDGS [233] Jer 17:5-10/ Lk 16:19-31
22 Fri - Lenten Weekday
Vi MASS pref I-IV of Lent
RDGS [234] Gn 37:3-4,12-13a,17b-28a/ Mt 21:33- 43,45-46
23 Sat - Lenten Weekday
Vi MASS pref I-IV of Lent
RDGS [235] Mi 7:14-15,18-20/ Lk 15:1-3,11-32
[*St. Turibius of Mogrovejo, Bishop*]

=============

24 Sun - **3rd SUNDAY OF LENT** HOURS Week III
Vi MASS cr, pref I or II of Lent [For Cycle A: prop pref]
RDGS [30] Ex 3:1-8a,13-15/ 1 Cor 10:1-6,10-12/ Lk 13:1-9
Or, when Year A rdgs are used: [28] Ex 17:3-7/ Rom 5:1-2,5-8/ Jn 4:5-42 or 4:5-15,19b-26,39a,40-42. If Year A rdgs are used, the prop pref for the Third Sunday of Lent may be used.

----

* On this Sunday is celebrated the first scrutiny in preparation for the Baptism of the catechumens who are to be admitted to the Sacraments of Christian Initiation at the Easter Vigil, using the proper prayers and intercessions in the **Roman Missal.**
* The optional Mass for the Third Week of Lent, [236] Ex 17:1-7/ Jn 4:5-12, may be used on any day of this week, especially in Years B and C when the Gospel of the Samaritan Woman is not read on the Third Sunday of Lent.
* EP = Second Vespers (Evening Prayer II) of The Third Sunday of Lent.

----

25 Mon - **THE ANNUNCIATION OF THE LORD (S)**
Wh MASS gl, cr, prop pref
RDGS [545] Is 7:10-14; 8:10/ Heb 10:4-10/ Lk 1:26-38
26 Tue - Lenten Weekday
Vi MASS pref I-IV of Lent
RDGS [238] Dn 3:25,34-43/ Mt 18:21-35

27 Wed - Lenten Weekday
Vi MASS pref I-IV of Lent
RDGS [239] Dt 4:1,5-9/ Mt 5:17-19
28 Thu - Lenten Weekday
Vi MASS pref I-IV of Lent
RDGS [240] Jer 7:23-28/ Lk 11:14-23
29 Fri - Lenten Weekday
Vi MASS pref I-IV of Lent
RDGS [241] Hos 14:2-10/ Mk 12:28-34
30 Sat - Lenten Weekday
Vi MASS pref I-IV of Lent
RDGS [242] Hos 6:1-6/ Lk 18:9-14

=============

31 Sun - **4th SUNDAY OF LENT** HOURS Week IV
Vi/Ro MASS cr, pref I or II of Lent [For Cycle A: prop pref]
RDGS [33] Jos 5:9a,10-12/ 2 Cor 5:17-21/ Lk 15:1-3,11-32
Or, when Year A rdgs are used: [31] 1 Sm 16:1b,6-7,10-13a/ Eph 5:8-14/ Jn 9:1-41 or 9:1,6-9,13-17,34-38. If Year A rdgs are used, the prop pref for the Fourth Sunday of Lent may be used.

---

* On this Sunday is celebrated the second scrutiny in preparation for the Baptism of the catechumens who are to be admitted to the Sacraments of Christian Initiation at the Easter Vigil, using the proper prayers and intercessions in the **Roman Missal**.
* The optional Mass for the Fourth Week of Lent, [243] Mi 7:7-9/ Jn 9:1-41, may be used on any day of this week, especially in Years B and C when the Gospel of the Man Born Blind is not read on the Fourth Sunday of Lent.

April 2019

1 Mon - Lenten Weekday
Vi MASS pref I-IV of Lent
RDGS [244] Is 65:17-21/ Jn 4:43-54
2 Tue - Lenten Weekday
Vi MASS pref I-IV of Lent
RDGS [245] Ez 47:1-9,12/ Jn 5:1-16
[*St. Francis of Paola, Hermit*]
3 Wed - Lenten Weekday
Vi MASS pref I-IV of Lent
RDGS [246] Is 49:8-15/ Jn 5:17-30

April

4 Thu - Lenten Weekday
Vi MASS pref I-IV of Lent
RDGS [247] Ex 32:7-14/ Jn 5:31-47
[*St. Isidore, Bishop and Doctor of the Church*]
[*St. Benedict, Religious - Nigeria*]

---

5 Fri - Lenten Weekday
Vi MASS pref I-IV of Lent
RDGS [248] Wis 2:1a,12-22/ Jn 7:1-2,10,25-30

6 Sat - Lenten Weekday
Vi MASS pref I-IV of Lent
RDGS [249] Jer 11:18-20/ Jn 7:40-53

---

* In the Dioceses of the United States, the practice of covering crosses and images throughout the church from this Sunday may be observed. Crosses remain covered until the end of the celebration of the Lord's Passion on Good Friday, but images remain covered until the beginning of the Easter Vigil.

=============

7 Sun - **5th SUNDAY OF LENT** HOURS Week I
Vi MASS cr, pref I or II of Lent [For Cycle A: prop pref]
RDGS [36] Is 43:16-21/ Phil 3:8-14/ Jn 8:1-11
Or, when Year A rdgs are used: [34] Ez 37:12-14/ Rom 8:8-11/ Jn 11:1-45 or 11:3-7,17,20-27, 33b-45. If Year A rdgs are used, the prop pref for the Fifth Sunday of Lent may be used.

---

* On this Sunday is celebrated the third scrutiny in preparation for the Baptism of the catechumens who are to be admitted to the Sacraments of Initiation at the Easter Vigil, using the proper prayers and intercessions in the **Roman Missal**.
* The optional Mass for the Fifth Week of Lent, [250] 2 Kgs 4:18b-21,32-37/ Jn 11:1-45, may be used on any day of this week, especially in years B and C when the Gospel of Lazarus is not read on the Fifth Sunday of Lent.

---

8 Mon - Lenten Weekday
Vi MASS pref I of the Passion of the Lord
RDGS [251] Dn 13:1-9,15-17,19-30,33-62 or 13:41c-62/ Jn 8:12-20 (2nd choice)

9 Tue - Lenten Weekday
Vi MASS pref I of the Passion of the Lord
RDGS [252] Nm 21:4-9/ Jn 8:21-30

10 Wed - Lenten Weekday
Vi MASS pref I of the Passion of the Lord
RDGS [253] Dn 3:14-20,91-92,95/ Jn 8:31-42

11 Thu - Lenten Weekday
Vi MASS pref I of the Passion of the Lord
RDGS [254] Gn 17:3-9/ Jn 8:51-59
[*St. Stanislaus, Bishop and Martyr*]
12 Fri - Lenten Weekday
Vi MASS pref I of the Passion of the Lord
RDGS [255] Jer 20:10-13/ Jn 10:31-42
[*St. Zeno of Verona, Bishop - Nigeria*]
13 Sat - Lenten Weekday
Vi MASS pref I of the Passion of the Lord
RDGS [256] Ez 37:21-28/ Jn 11:45-56
[*St. Martin I, Pope and Martyr*]

=============

14 Sun - **PALM SUNDAY OF THE PASSION OF THE LORD**
HOURS Week II
Rd PROCESSION [37] Lk 19:28-40
MASS cr, prop pref
RDGS [38] Is 50:4-7/ Phil 2:6-11/ Lk 22:14–23:56 or 23:1-49

OP 1. On this day the Church recalls the entrance of Christ the Lord into Jerusalem to accomplish his Paschal Mystery. Accordingly, the memorial of this entrance of the Lord takes place at all Masses, by means of the Procession or Solemn Entrance before the conventual Mass or the Simple Entrance before other Masses. The Solemn Entrance, but not the Procession, may be repeated before other Masses that are usually celebrated with a large gathering of people.

2. Palms may be distributed either when all are gathered or immediately after the blessing before the proclamation of the Gospel, i.e., the Gospel of the Procession.

3. After the Procession or Solemn Entrance, the greeting and Penitential Act or the blessing and sprinkling of water and, if appropriate, the *Kyrie* (Lord, have mercy) are omitted and the Collect of the Mass concludes the procession; Mass continues in the usual way.

4. The narrative of the Lord's Passion is read without candles and without incense, with no greeting or signing of the book. It is read by a Deacon or, if there is no Deacon, by a Concelebrant or the Principal Celebrant himself. It may also be read by readers, whether religious (brothers cooperator, nuns and sisters) or lay, with the part of Christ, if possible, reserved to a Deacon or a Priest. Deacons, but not others, ask for the blessing of the Principal Celebrant before singing the Passion, as at other times before the Gospel.

* The Mass for Palm Sunday is provided with three readings. It is strongly recommended that all three be used, unless pastoral reasons suggest otherwise.
Given, however, the importance of the account of the Lord's Passion, the Priest, having in mind the character of each individual congregation, is authorized to choose only one of the two readings prescribed before the Gospel or, if necessary, he may read only the account of the Passion, even in the shorter form. This permission applies, however, only to Masses celebrated with a congregation.
The Passion begins directly, without the greeting or the acclamation of the people, but concludes in the usual manner.

----

15 Mon - **MONDAY OF HOLY WEEK**
Vi Mass pref II of the Passion of the Lord
RDGS [257] Is 42:1-7/ Jn 12:1-11

16 Tue - **TUESDAY OF HOLY WEEK**
Vi MASS pref II of the Passion of the Lord
RDGS [258] Is 49:1-6/ Jn 13:21-33,36-38

17 Wed - **WEDNESDAY OF HOLY WEEK**
Vi MASS pref II of the Passion of the Lord
RDGS [259] Is 50:4-9a/ Mt 26:14-25

THURSDAY OF HOLY WEEK

OP If appropriate, today or on another day of this week, following the tradition of the Order, in place of the ancient rite of the Penitential Psalms some communal penitential celebration or "rite of reconciliation" may take place,– whether it be sacramental or non-sacramental – according to the spirit of the **Rite of Penance** (nn.36-37) and the norms of liturgical law. However, this celebration may not immediately precede Mass.

THE EASTER TRIDUUM

OP 1. The Easter Triduum of the Passion and Resurrection of Christ is the culmination of the entire liturgical year. (RC, n.18)
2. The Easter Triduum begins with the Evening Mass of the Lord's Supper, reaches its high point in the Easter Vigil, and closes with Vespers (Evening Prayer) on Easter Sunday. (RC, n.19)
3. During these days it is desirable that brothers and sisters who are sick, especially those in hospitals, should be helped to consider the meaning of sickness which is lived in union with the Paschal Mystery of Christ. For this reason, the sick should share in or be participants in the liturgical celebrations of the community.
4. Therefore, keeping in mind their varying and different circumstances, everything should be so arranged that in a more suitable manner the sick may have the possibility of receiving Communion and, if possible, participating in the Adoration of the Cross on Good Friday. The various faculties found in the Ritual should be freely used.

Indeed our concern, which is manifested through our care and our prayer, furnishes the strongest witness to the mutual bonds by which we are united by the Gospel concerning our faith in God and the power of the Resurrection of his Son.

* In accordance with a most ancient tradition of the Church, on this day all Masses without the people are forbidden. Where a pastoral reason requires it, the local Ordinary may permit another Mass to be celebrated in churches and oratories in the evening and in case of genuine necessity, even in the morning, but only for the faithful who are in no way able to participate in the evening Mass.

----

18 Thu - **THURSDAY OF HOLY WEEK (Holy Thursday)**

Wh EVENING MASS OF THE LORD'S SUPPER

gl, pref I of the Most Holy Eucharist, *prop Roman Canon inserts*

RDGS [39] Ex 12:1-8,11-14/ 1 Cor 11:23-26/ Jn 13:1-15

OP 1. The rite of the *Mandatum* may be celebrated by the friars outside Mass in the chapter room, or in the cloister, or in another suitable place.

While the *Mandatum* is carried out, the Gospel may be read (Jn 13:1-17 or some other excerpt from Jn 13-17) and some of the customary chants for the *Mandatum* (see **OHS**, pp.91-98) or other appropriate chants may be sung.

2. The *Sermo Dominicus* (Jn 13:1-14:31) may be used at table in the vernacular or as the last celebration of the day. In this case it is read in place of Compline (Night Prayer) with the community gathered before the Blessed Sacrament.

3. At a suitable time after the celebration of this day is concluded, the altar is stripped and, if possible, crosses are removed from the church. It is desirable to cover any crosses which remain in the church. Holy water is removed from containers in the church.

4. A major prelate presides at the principal hours of the Office and at Mass. The principal hours of the Office begin on the right side of choir.

----

19 Fri - **FRIDAY OF THE PASSION OF THE LORD (Good Friday)**

Rd CELEBRATION OF THE PASSION OF THE LORD

RDGS [40] Is 52:13–53:12/ Heb 4:14-16; 5:7-9/ Jn 18:1–19:42

OP 1. On Good Friday and, if possible, also on Holy Saturday until the Easter Vigil, the Easter fast is observed everywhere. (RC, n.20)

2. Today and tomorrow at the conclusion of Lauds (Morning Prayer) in place of the intercessions found in the **Liturgy of the Hours** the *Versus litanici* may be sung, either in Latin with the Gregorian melodies (see **OHS**, pp.60-63) or in the vernacular using suitable melodies composed for them. At the end, after a pause for silence, the Lord's Prayer is said aloud as is the custom at the end of Lauds (Morning Prayer).

3. The special rite for the Adoration of the Cross (as found in the **Missale et Lectionarium OP** (1985), pp.36-43) may be used, observing the adaptations of the restored liturgy regarding the ministers, the color of vestments (red) and the way such special elements fit into the ritual action as a whole. The verses for the Reproaches (*Popule meus, Quid eduxi, Quid ultra*) may be sung with the help of cantors or, if necessary, simply proclaimed.
4. Compline (Night Prayer) is said after the Celebration of the Passion of the Lord at a suitable hour. Two candles are lit.

NOTE:
a) Today and tomorrow at the Office of Readings and Lauds (Morning Prayer), candles may be lit only at the altar in the usual manner, the number and manner conforming to that of Solemnities. They remain lit during the entire Office.
b) At a suitable time the altar is stripped; however, the cross remains.
c) Today after the Adoration of the Cross the brothers, when entering and leaving choir, bow profoundly to the cross as on other days, but they do not genuflect.
d) Today the *De profundis* for deceased brothers and benefactors and the *Fidelium* are omitted at grace for meals. The custom of wearing the cappa in the refectory, where it exists, may be observed, unless it seems expedient to do otherwise.

----

20 Sat - **HOLY SATURDAY**

Wh EASTER VIGIL IN THE HOLY NIGHT

gl, Easter pref I, *prop Roman Canon inserts*

RDGS [41] Gn 1:1–2:2 or 1:1,26-31a/ Gn 22:1-18 or 22:1-2, 9a,10-13,15-18/ Ex 14:15–15:1/ Is 54:5-14/ Is 55:1-11/ Bar 3:9-15, 32–4:4/ Ez 36:16-17a,18-28/ Rom 6:3-11/ Lk 24:1-12

OP 1. The entire celebration of this Easter Vigil must take place during the night so that it begins after nightfall and ends before daybreak on the Sunday. (Cf. RC, n.21)
2. In this holy Vigil the Easter Proclamation (*Exultet*) can be sung with the proper melody found in the **Missale et Lectionarium OP** (1985), pp.492-498, in either the longer or shorter form.
3. The Easter Proclamation, if necessary, may be sung even by a cantor who is not a Deacon, e.g., nuns in their own monasteries. In this case, however, the cantor omits the words "Therefore, dearest friends" up to the end of the invitation along with the greeting "The Lord be with you."

* The paschal candle remains lit in all the more solemn liturgical celebrations of this period.
* Nine readings are assigned to the Easter Vigil: seven from the Old Testament and two from the New. If circumstances demand in individual cases, the number of prescribed readings may be reduced. Three selections from the Old Testament, however, should be read before the Epistle and Gospel, although when necessary two may be read. In any case, the reading from Exodus about the escape through the Red Sea (reading 3) should never be omitted.

21 Sun - **EASTER SUNDAY OF THE RESURRECTION OF THE LORD (S)**
MASS DURING THE DAY HOURS Week I
Wh MASS gl, seq, renewal of baptismal promises, pref I of Easter, *prop Roman Canon inserts*
RDGS [42] Acts 10:34a,37-43/ Col 3:1-4 or 1 Cor 5:6b-8/ Jn 20:1-9 or [41] Lk 24:1-12. At an evening Mass the following Gospel may be read: [46] Lk 24:13-35.

----

* In Easter Sunday Masses which are celebrated with a congregation, the rite of the renewal of baptismal promises may take place after the Homily, according to the text used at the Easter Vigil. In that case the Creed is omitted.
* The Easter Triduum concludes with the celebration of Vespers (Evening Prayer). The fifty-day celebration of Easter then begins, concluding with Pentecost Sunday.

OP After Compline (Night Prayer) the paschal candle is extinguished. It is lit throughout Easter Time at Mass and at the principal hours of the Office up to and including Pentecost Sunday.

----

22 Mon - **MONDAY WITHIN THE OCTAVE OF EASTER (S)**
Wh MASS gl, pref I of Easter, *prop Roman Canon inserts*
RDGS [261] Acts 2:14,22-32/ Mt 28:8-15

23 Tue - **TUESDAY WITHIN THE OCTAVE OF EASTER (S)**
Wh MASS gl, pref I of Easter, *prop Roman Canon inserts*
RDGS [262] Acts 2:36-41/ Jn 20:11-18

24 Wed - **WEDNESDAY WITHIN THE OCTAVE OF EASTER (S)**
Wh MASS gl, pref I of Easter, *prop Roman Canon inserts*
RDGS [263] Acts 3:1-10/ Lk 24:13-35

25 Thu - **THURSDAY WITHIN THE OCTAVE OF EASTER (S)**
Wh MASS gl, pref I of Easter, *prop Roman Canon inserts*
RDGS [264] Acts 3:11-26/ Lk 24:35-48

26 Fri - **FRIDAY WITHIN THE OCTAVE OF EASTER (S)**
Wh MASS gl, pref I of Easter, *prop Roman Canon inserts*
RDGS [265] Acts 4:1-12/ Jn 21:1-14

27 Sat - **SATURDAY WITHIN THE OCTAVE OF EASTER (S)**
Wh MASS gl, pref I of Easter, *prop Roman Canon inserts*
RDGS [266] Acts 4:13-21/ Mk 16:9-15

=============

28 Sun - **2nd SUNDAY OF EASTER (or SUNDAY OF DIVINE MERCY) (S)**
HOURS Week II
Wh MASS gl, cr, pref I of Easter, *prop Roman Canon inserts*
RDGS [45] Acts 5:12-16/ Rv 1:9-11a.12-13,17-19/ Jn 20:19-31

29 Mon - **St. Catherine of Siena, OP, Virgin and Doctor of the Church (F)**
Wh MASS gl, cr, prop pref
RDGS Prop: Rv 1:5-8 [970.3] or Col 1:24-29 [722.9] or 1 Jn 1:5–2:2 [949.2]/ Ps 103 [739.6] or Ps 22 [924.1]/ Jn 7:14-18,37-39 or Jn 17:1-11a [871.6] or Jn 14:21-26 [285]
30 Tue - St. Pius V, OP, Pope (M)
Wh MASS pref I-V of Easter
RDGS [268] Acts 4:32-37/ Jn 3:7b-15
As above, or, prop: Acts 20:17-18a,28-32,36 [720.2] or 1 Cor 2:1-10a [728.2]/ Ps 110 [558]/ Jn 21:15-17 [558] or Lk 22:28-32

EA For the Vicariate of Eastern Africa (Eastern Province) and
JW For the Province of St. Joseph the Worker:
30 - **Our Lady, Mother of Africa (F)**
Wh MASS gl, pref I or II of BVM
RDGS prop

May 2019

1 Wed - Easter Weekday
Wh MASS pref I-V of Easter
RDGS [269] Acts 5:17-26/ Jn 3:16-21
[*Wh - St. Joseph the Worker*]
MASS prop pref
RDGS [559] Gn 1:26–2:3 or Col 3:14-15,17,23-24/ Mt 13:54-58

JW Titular feast of the Province of St. Joseph the Worker:
1 - **St. Joseph the Worker (F)**
Wh MASS gl, pref of St. Joseph
RDGS [559] Gn 1:26–2:3 or Col 3:14-15,17,23-24/ Mt 13:54-58

----

2 Thu - St. Athanasius, Bishop and Doctor of the Church (M)
Wh MASS pref I-V of Easter
RDGS [270] Acts 5:27-33/ Jn 3:31-36
3 Fri - **SS. Philip and James, Apostles (F)**
Rd MASS gl, pref I or II of Apostles
RDGS [561] 1 Cor 15:1-8/ Jn 14:6-14
4 Sat - Easter Weekday
Wh MASS pref I-V of Easter
RDGS [272] Acts 6:1-7/ Jn 6:16-21

=============

5 Sun - **3rd SUNDAY OF EASTER** HOURS Week III

Wh MASS gl, cr, pref I-V of Easter

RDGS [48] Acts 5:27-32,40b-41/ Rv 5:11-14/ Jn 21:1-19 or 21:1-14

6 Mon -Easter Weekday

Wh MASS pref I-V of Easter

RDGS [273] Acts 6:8-15/ Jn 6:22-29

7 Tue - Easter Weekday

Wh MASS pref I-V of Easter

RDGS [274] Acts 7:51–8:1a/ Jn 6:30-35

8 Wed - Easter Weekday

Wh MASS pref I-V of Easter

RDGS [275] Acts 8:1b-8/ Jn 6:35-40

OP To recall the patronage of the Blessed Virgin Mary over the whole Order of Preachers, today the Consecration to the Blessed Virgin Mary may be renewed using the formula from the General Chapter of 1974. (The text of this consecration may be found on p.31).

If there is good reason for it, on another appropriate day a Votive Mass of the Blessed Virgin Mary may be celebrated using the special votive Mass proper to the Order.

[*Wh - Patronage of the Blessed Virgin Mary*]

MASS pref I or II of BVM

RDGS Prop: (A) Eph 1:3-6,16-19 [710.4]/ Resp. Ps [572]/ Lk 1:39-47 [712.5] or (B) Eph 3:14-19 [740.7]/ Ps 16 [739.3]/ Jn 19:25-27 [712.12]

---

9 Thu - Easter Weekday

Wh MASS pref I-V of Easter

RDGS [276] Acts 8:26-40/ Jn 6:44-51

10 Fri - St. Antoninus Pierozzi of Florence, OP, Bishop (M)

Wh MASS pref I-V of Easter

RDGS [277] Acts 9:1-20/ Jn 6:52-59

As above, or, prop: Sir 37:16-25 or Jas 3:13-18 [883.9]/ Ps 119 [727.3]/ Lk 12:35-44 [774.6]

11 Sat - Easter Weekday

Wh MASS pref I-V of Easter

RDGS [278] Acts 9:31-42/ Jn 6:60-69

=============

12 Sun - **4th SUNDAY OF EASTER** HOURS Week IV

Wh MASS gl, cr, pref I-V of Easter

RDGS [51] Acts 13:14,43-52/ Rv 7:9,14b-17/ Jn 10:27-30

13 Mon -Easter Weekday
Wh MASS pref I-V of Easter
RDGS [279] Acts 11:1-18/ Jn 10:1-10 (1st choice)
[*Wh - Our Lady of Fatima*]
MASS pref I or II of BVM
14 Tue - **St. Matthias, Apostle (F)**
Rd MASS gl, pref I or II of Apostles
RDGS [564] Acts 1:15-17,20-26/ Jn 15:9-17
15 Wed - Easter Weekday
Wh MASS pref I-V of Easter
RDGS [281] Acts 12:24–13:5a/ Jn 12:44-50
[*Wh - St. Isidore - USA*]
16 Thu - Easter Weekday
Wh MASS pref I-V of Easter
RDGS [282] Acts 13:13-25/ Jn 13:16-20
17 Fri - Easter Weekday
Wh MASS pref I-V of Easter
RDGS [283] Acts 13:26-33/ Jn 14:1-6
18 Sat - Easter Weekday
Wh MASS pref I-V of Easter
RDGS [284] Acts 13:44-52/ Jn 14:7-14
[*Rd - St. John I, Pope and Martyr*]

=============

19 Sun - **5th SUNDAY OF EASTER** HOURS Week I
Wh MASS gl, cr, pref I-V of Easter
RDGS [54] Acts 14:21-27/ Rv 21:1-5a/ Jn 13:31-33a,34-35
20 Mon - Easter Weekday
Wh MASS pref I-V of Easter
RDGS [285] Acts 14:5-18/ Jn 14:21-26
[*Wh - St. Bernardine of Siena, Priest*]
21 Tue - Easter Weekday
Wh MASS pref I-V of Easter
RDGS [286] Acts 14:19-28/ Jn 14:27-31a
[*Rd - St. Christopher Magallanes, Priest, and Companions, Martyrs*]
[*Wh - Bl. Hyacinthe-Marie Cormier, OP, Priest*]
RDGS As above, or, prop: 1 Jn 5:1-5 [740.18]/ Ps 16 [721.1]/ Lk 14:25-53 [742.23]

22 Wed - Easter Weekday
Wh MASS pref I-V of Easter
RDGS [287] Acts 15:1-6/ Jn 15:1-8
[*Wh - St. Rita of Cascia, Religious*]
23 Thu - Easter Weekday
Wh MASS pref I-V of Easter
RDGS [288] Acts 15:7-21/ Jn 15:9-11
24 Fri - The Translation of Holy Father Dominic (M)
Wh MASS *seq*, prop pref
RDGS [289] Acts 15:22-31/ Jn 15:12-17
As above, or, prop: Acts 4:32-35 [812.2]/ Ps 16 [721.1] or Ps 96 [721.5]/ Mt 28:16-20 [724.4]
25 Sat - Easter Weekday
Wh MASS pref I-V of Easter
RDGS [290] Acts 16:1-10/ Jn 15:18-21
[*Wh - St. Bede the Venerable, Priest and Doctor of the Church*]
[*Wh - St. Gregory VII, Pope*]
[*Wh - St. Mary Magdalene de' Pazzi, Virgin*]

=============

26 Sun - **6th SUNDAY OF EASTER** HOURS Week II
Wh MASS gl, cr, pref I-V of Easter
RDGS [57] Acts 15:1-2,22-29/ Rv 21:10-14,22-23/ Jn 14:23-29

---

* When The Ascension of the Lord is celebrated on the following Sunday, the Second Reading and Gospel of the Seventh Sunday of Easter [see 61] may be read on the Sixth Sunday of Easter.

---

27 Mon - Easter Weekday
Wh MASS pref I-V of Easter
RDGS [291] Acts 16:11-15/ Jn 15:26–16:4a
[*Wh - St. Augustine of Canterbury, Bishop*]
28 Tue - Easter Weekday
Wh MASS pref I-V of Easter
RDGS [292] Acts 16:22-34/ Jn 16:5-11
29 Wed - Easter Weekday
Wh MASS pref I-V of Easter
RDGS [293] Acts 17:15,22–18:1/ Jn 16:12-15

---

* When The Ascension of the Lord is observed on Thursday, EP = First Vespers (Evening Prayer I) of The Ascension of the Lord.

FOR THE ECCLESIASTICAL PROVINCES OF BOSTON, HARTFORD, NEW YORK, NEWARK, OMAHA, AND PHILADELPHIA:

30 Thu - **THE ASCENSION OF THE LORD (S)**

Wherever in the United States The Ascension of the Lord is observed today, it is a holy day of obligation.

Wh MASS gl, cr, pref I or II of the Ascen, *prop Roman Canon inserts*

RDGS [58] Acts 1:1-11/ Eph 1:17-23 or Heb 9:24-28; 10:19-23/ Lk 24:46-53

OP The weekdays from the Ascension up to and including the Saturday before Pentecost prepare for the coming of the Holy Spirit, the Paraclete. (RC, n.26)

* The preface for Easter Weekdays from Thursday through Saturday of this week for these Provinces is: pref I-V or pref I or II of Ascen.

ALL OTHER U.S. ECCLESIASTICAL PROVINCES:

30 Thu - Easter Weekday

Wh MASS pref I-V of Easter

RDGS [294] Acts 18:1-18/ Jn 16:16-20

----

* The preface for Easter Weekdays from Thursday through Saturday of this week for these Provinces is: pref I-V of Easter.

31 Fri - **The Visitation of the Blessed Virgin Mary (F)**

Wh MASS gl, pref I or II of BVM

RDGS [572] Zep 3:14-18a or Rom 12:9-16/ Lk 1:39-56

June 2019

1 Sat - St. Justin, Martyr (M)

Rd MASS pref I-V of Easter [or pref I or II of Ascen]

RDGS [296] Acts 18:23-28/ Jn 16:23b-28

----

* Wherever The Ascension of the Lord is observed on the Seventh Sunday of Easter: EP = First Vespers (Evening Prayer I) of The Ascension of the Lord.

=============

FOR THE ECCLESIASTICAL PROVINCES OF BOSTON, HARTFORD, NEW YORK, NEWARK, OMAHA, AND PHILADELPHIA:

2 Sun - **7th SUNDAY OF EASTER** HOURS Week III
Wh MASS gl, cr, pref I-V of Easter or pref I or II of Ascen
RDGS [61] Acts 7:55-60/ Rv 22:12-14,16-17,20/ Jn 17:20-26

ALL OTHER U.S. ECCLESIASTICAL PROVINCES:

2 Sun - **THE ASCENSION OF THE LORD (S)** HOURS Week III
Wh MASS gl, cr, pref I or II of Ascen, *prop Roman Canon inserts*
RDGS [58] Acts 1:1-11/ Eph 1:17-23 or Heb 9:24-28; 10:19-23/ Lk 24:46-53

3 Mon - St. Charles Lwanga and Companions, Martyrs (M)
Rd MASS pref I-V of Easter or pref I or II of Ascen
RDGS [297] Acts 19:1-8/ Jn 16:29-33
4 Tue - St. Peter of Verona, OP, Priest (M)
Rd MASS prop pref
RDGS [298] Acts 20:17-27/ Jn 17:1-11a
As above, or, prop: 2 Tm 2:3-13 or Acts 7:55-60 [714.1]/ Ps 31 [715.1]/ Jn 15:18-21 [718.6] or Lk 12:4-9
5 Wed - St. Boniface, Bishop and Martyr (M)
Rd MASS pref I-V of Easter or pref I or II of Ascen
RDGS [299] Acts 20:28-38/ Jn 17:11b-19
6 Thu - Easter Weekday
Wh MASS pref I-V of Easter or pref I or II of Ascen
RDGS [300] Acts 22:30; 23:6-11/ Jn 17:20-26
[*Wh - St. Norbert, Bishop*]
7 Fri -Easter Weekday
Wh MASS pref I-V of Easter or pref I or II of Ascen
RDGS [301] Acts 25:13b-21/ Jn 21:15-19
8 Sat - Easter Weekday
Wh MASS pref I-V of Easter or pref I or II of Ascen
RDGS [302] Acts 28:16-20,30-31/ Jn 21:20-25
[*Bl. Diana Andaló, OP, and Bl. Cecilia, OP, Virgins*]
Wh RDGS As above, or, prop: Col 3:1-4 [812.10]/ Os 63 [813.8]/ Mt 25:1-13 [815.6]

----

* EP = First Vespers (Evening Prayer I) of Pentecost Sunday.

=============

9 Sun - **PENTECOST SUNDAY (S)** HOURS Week II

Rd MASS gl, seq, cr, pref of Pentecost, *prop Roman Canon inserts*

RDGS Vigil: [62] Gn 11:1-9 or Ex 19:3-8a,16-20b or Ez 37:1-14 or Jl 3:1-5/ Rom 8:22-27/ Jn 7:37-39

Extended Vigil: [62] Gn 11:1-9/ Ex 19:3-8a,16-20b/ Ez 37:1-14 / Jl 3:1-5/ Rom 8:22-27/ Jn 7:37-39

Day: [63] Acts 2:1-11/ 1 Cor 12:3b-7,12-13 or Rom 8:8-17/ Jn 20:19-23 or Jn 14:15-16,23b-26

----

* The Vigil Mass may be celebrated on Saturday evening, either before or after First Vespers (Evening Prayer I) of Pentecost Sunday; it may be celebrated in an extended form as provided in the **Roman Missal**.

* Easter Time concludes with Second Vespers (Evening Prayer II) of Pentecost.

----

10 Mon - The Blessed Virgin Mary, Mother of the Church (M)

(10th Week in Ordinary Time)

Wh MASS **Roman Missal**, Votive Masses 10/B - "Our Lady, Mother of the Church"; pref I or II of BVM

RDGS From *Lectionary for Mass Supplement* [572A] Gn 3:9-15,20 or Acts 1:12-14/ Ps 87/ Jn 19:25-34

11 Tue - St. Barnabas, Apostle (M)

Rd MASS pref I or II of Apostles

RDGS [580] Acts 11:21b-26; 13:1-3/ [360] Mt 5:13-16

12 Wed - Weekday

Gr RDGS [361] 2 Cor 3:4-11/ Mt 5:17-19

[*Wh - St. Onophrius, Hermit - Nigeria*]

13 Thu - St. Anthony of Padua, Priest and Doctor of the Church (M)

Wh RDGS [362] 2 Cor 3:15–4:1,3-6/ Mt 5:20-26

14 Fri - Weekday

Gr RDGS [363] 2 Cor 4:7-15/ Mt 5:27-32

15 Sat - Weekday

Gr RDGS [364] 2 Cor 5:14-21/ Mt 5:33-37

[*Wh - BVM on Sat or OP Votive Mass*]

MASS pref I or II of BVM

RDGS as above or OP Votive Mass

=============

16 Sun - **THE MOST HOLY TRINITY (S)** HOURS Week III
Wh MASS gl, cr, prop pref
RDGS [166] Prv 8:22-31/ Rom 5:1-5/ Jn 16:12-15
17 Mon - Weekday (11the Week in Ordinary Time)
Gr RDGS [365] 2 Cor 6:1-10/ Mt 5:38-42
18 Tue - Weekday
Gr RDGS [366] 2 Cor 8:1-9/ Mt 5:43-48
19 Wed - Weekday
Gr RDGS [367] 2 Cor 9:6-11/ Mt 6:1-6,16-18
[*Wh - St. Romuald, Abbot*]
20 Thu - Weekday
Gr RDGS [368] 2 Cor 11:1-11/ Mt 6:7-15
21 Fri - St. Aloysius Gonzaga, Religious (M)
Wh RDGS [369] 2 Cor 11:18,21-30/ Mt 6:19-23
22 Sat -Weekday
Gr RDGS [370] 2 Cor 12:1-10/ Mt 6:24-34
[*Wh - St. Paulinus of Nola, Bishop*]
[*Rd - SS. John Fisher, Bishop, and Thomas More, Martyrs*]
[*Wh - BVM on Sat or OP Votive Mass*]
MASS pref I or II of BVM
RDGS as above or OP Votive Mass

=============

23 Sun - **THE MOST HOLY BODY AND BLOOD OF CHRIST**

(Corpus Christi) (S)
HOURS Week IV
Wh MASS gl, *seq*, cr, pref I or II of the Most Holy Eucharist
RDGS [169] Gn 14:18-20/ 1 Cor 11:23-26/ Lk 9:11b-17

----

* EP = Second Vespers (Evening Prayer II) of The Most Holy Body and Blood of Christ.

----

24 Mon - **THE NATIVITY OF ST. JOHN THE BAPTIST (S)**
Wh MASS gl, cr, prop pref
RDGS Vigil: [586] Jer 1:4-10/ 1 Pt 1:8-12/ Lk 1:5-17
Day: [587] Is 49:1-6/ Acts 13:22-26/ Lk 1:57- 66,80
25 Tue - Weekday (12th Week in Ordinary Time)
Gr RDGS [372] Gn 13:2,5-18/ Mt 7:6,12-14
26 Wed - Weekday
Gr RDGS [373] Gn 15:1-12,17-18/ Mt 7:15-20

27 Thu -Weekday
Gr RDGS [374] Gn 16:1-12,15-16 or 16:6b-12,15-16/ Mt 7:21-29
[*Wh - St. Cyril of Alexandria, Bishop and Doctor of the Church*]

---

* EP = First Vespers (Evening Prayer I) of The Most Sacred Heart of Jesus.

---

28 Fri - **THE MOST SACRED HEART OF JESUS (S)**
Wh MASS gl, cr, prop pref
RDGS [172] Ez 34:11-16/ Rom 5:5b-11/ Lk 15:3-7

---

* EP = Second Vespers (Evening Prayer II) of The Most Sacred Heart of Jesus.

---

29 Sat - **SS. PETER and PAUL, Apostles (S)**
Rd MASS gl, cr, prop pref
RDGS Vigil: [590] Acts 3:1-10/ Gal 1:11-20/ Jn 21:15-19
Day: [591] Acts 12:1-11/ 2 Tm 4:6-8,17-18/ Mt 16:13-19

---

* EP = Second Vespers (Evening Prayer II) of SS. Peter and Paul.

=============

30 Sun - **13th Sunday in Ordinary Time** HOURS Week I
Gr MASS gl, cr, pref I-VIII of Sundays in Ordinary Time
RDGS [99] 1 Kgs 19:16b,19-21/ Gal 5:1,13-18/ Lk 9:51-62

JULY 2019

1 Mon - Weekday
Gr RDGS [377] Gn 18:16-33/ Mt 8:18-22
[*Wh - St. Junípero Sera, Priest - USA*]
2 Tue - Weekday
Gr RDGS [378] Gn 19:15-29/ Mt 8:23-27
3 Wed - **St. Thomas, Apostle (F)**
Rd MASS gl, pref I or II of Apostles
RDGS [593] Eph 2:19-22/ Jn 20:24-29
4 Thu - Weekday
Gr RDGS [380] Gn 22:1b-19/ Mt 9:1-8
[*Wh - Independence Day (National Holiday - USA)*]
MASS gl, prop pref
RDGS [594A] Any rdgs from the Mass "For the Country or a City" [882-886] or "For Peace and Justice" [887-891]
[*Wh - St. Elizabeth of Portugal - Nigeria*]

5 Fri - Weekday
Gr RDGS [381] Gn 23:1-4,19; 24:1-8,62-67/ Mt 9:9-13
[*Wh - St. Anthony Zaccaria, Priest*]
[*Wh - St. Elizabeth of Portugal - USA*]
6 Sat - Weekday
Gr RDGS [382] Gn 27:1-5,15-29/ Mt 9:14-17
[*Rd - St. Maria Goretti, Virgin and Martyr*]
[*Wh - BVM on Sat or OP Votive Mass*]
MASS pref I or II of BVM
RDGS as above or OP Votive Mass

=============

7 Sun - **14th Sunday in Ordinary Time** HOURS Week II
Gr MASS gl, cr, pref I-VIII of Sundays in Ordinary Time
RDGS [102] Is 66:10-14c/ Gal 6:14-18/ Lk 10:1-12,17-20 or 10:1-9
8 Mon - Weekday
Gr RDGS [383] Gn 28:10-22a/ Mt 9:18-26
9 Tue - St. John of Cologne, OP, Priest, and Companions, Martyrs (M)
Rd RDGS [384] Gn 32:23-33/ Mt 9:32-38
As above, or, prop: Wis 10:9-12 or 2 Cor 6:4-10 [716.4]/ Ps 126 [715.4]/ Lk 6:22-28
10 Wed - Weekday
Gr RDGS [385] Gn 41:55-57; 42:5-7a,17-24a/ Mt 10:1-7
11 Thu - St. Benedict, Abbot (M)
Wh RDGS [386] Gn 44:18-21,23b-29; 45:1-5/ Mt 10:7-15
12 Fri - Weekday
Gr RDGS [387] Gn 46:1-7,28-30/ Mt 10:16-23
13 Sat - Weekday
Gr RDGS [388] Gn 49:29-32; 50:15-26a/ Mt 10:24-33
[*Wh - St. Henry*]
[*Wh - BVM on Sat or OP Votive Mass*]
MASS pref I or II of BVM
RDGS as above or OP Votive Mass

=============

14 Sun - **15th Sunday in Ordinary Time** HOURS Week III
Gr MASS gl, cr, pref I-VIII of Sundays in Ordinary Time
RDGS [105] Dt 30:10-14/ Col 1:15-20/ Lk 10:25-37
15 Mon - St. Bonaventure, Bishop and Doctor of the Church (M)
Wh RDGS [389] Ex 1:8-14,22/ Mt 10:34–11:1

16 Tue - Weekday
Gr RDGS [390] Ex 2:1-15a/ Mt 11:20-24
[*Wh - Our Lady of Mount Carmel*]
MASS pref I or II of BVM
17 Wed - Weekday
Gr RDGS [391] Ex 3:1-6,9-12/ Mt 11:25-27
[*Wh - Bl. Ceslaus of Poland, OP, Priest*]
RDGS As above, or, prop: 1 Tm 2:1-8 [873.6]/ Ps 67[874.2]/ Lk 24:44-53 [876.3]
18 Thu - Weekday
Gr RDGS [392] Ex 3:13-20/ Mt 11:28-30
[*Wh - St. Camillus de Lellis, Priest - USA*]
19 Fri - Weekday
Gr RDGS [393] Ex 11:10–12:14/ Mt 12:1-8
20 Sat - Weekday
Gr RDGS [394] Ex 12:37-42/ Mt 12:14-21
[*Rd - St. Apollinaris, Bishop and Martyr*]
[*Wh - BVM on Sat or OP Votive Mass*]
MASS pref I or II of BVM
RDGS as above or OP Votive Mass

=============

21 Sun - **16th Sunday in Ordinary Time** HOURS Week IV
Gr MASS gl, cr, pref I-VIII of Sundays in Ordinary Time
RDGS [108] Gn 18:1-10a/ Col 1:24-28/ Lk 10:38-42
22 Mon - St. Mary Magdalene (M)
Wh MASS gl, pref I or II of Saints
RDGS [603] Sg 3:1-4b or 2 Cor 5:14-17/ Jn 20:1-2,11-18
23 Tue - Weekday
Gr RDGS [396] Ex 14:21–15:1/ Mt 12:46-50
[*Wh - St. Bridget, Religious*]
24 Wed - Weekday
Gr RDGS [397] Ex 16:1-5,9-15/ Mt 13:1-9
[*Wh - St. Sharbel Makhlūf, Priest*]
25 Thu - **St. James, Apostle (F)**
Rd MASS gl, pref I or II of Apostles
RDGS [605] 2 Cor 4:7-15/ Mt 20:20-28
26 Fri - SS. Joachim and Anne, Parents of the Blessed Virgin Mary (M)
Wh RDGS [399] Ex 20:1-17/ Mt 13:18-23

27 Sat - Weekday
Gr RDGS [400] Ex 24:3-8/ Mt 13:24-30
[*Wh - BVM on Sat or OP Votive Mass*]
MASS pref I or II of BVM
RDGS as above or OP Votive Mass

=============

28 Sun - **17th Sunday in Ordinary Time** HOURS Week I
Gr MASS gl, cr, pref I-VIII of Sundays in Ordinary Time
RDGS [111] Gn 18:20-32/ Col 2:12-14/ Lk 11:1-13
29 Mon - St. Martha (M)
Wh RDGS [401] Ex 32:15-24,30-34/ [607] Jn 11:19-27 or Lk 10:38-42
30 Tue - Weekday
Gr RDGS [402] Ex 33:7-11; 34:5b-9,28/ Mt 13:36-43
[*Wh - St. Peter Chrysologus, Bishop and Doctor of the Church*]
[*Wh - St. Justin de Jacobis, Bishop - Nigeria*]
31 Wed - St. Ignatius of Loyola, Priest (M)
Wh RDGS [403] Ex 34:29-35/ Mt 13:44-46

AUGUST 2019

1 Thu - St. Alphonsus Liguori, Bishop and Doctor of the Church (M)
Wh RDGS [404] Ex 40:16-21,34-38/ Mt 13:47-53
2 Fri - Weekday
Gr RDGS [405] Lv 23:1,4-11,15-16,27,34b-37/ Mt 13:54-58
[*Wh - St. Eusebius of Vercelli, Bishop*]
[*Wh - St. Peter Julian Eymard, Priest*]
[*Wh - Bl. Jane of Aza, Mother of our Holy Father Dominic*]
RDGSAs above, or, prop: 1 Pt 4:7b-11 [740.15]/ Ps 131 [739.9]/ Mk 3:31-35 [742.14]
3 Sat - Weekday
Gr RDGS [406] Lv 25:1,8-17/ Mt 14:1-12
[*Wh - BVM on Sat or OP Votive Mass*]
MASS pref I or II of BVM
RDGS As above or OP Votive Mass

=============

4 Sun - **18th Sunday in Ordinary Time** HOURS Week II
Gr MASS gl, cr, pref I-VIII of Sundays in Ordinary Time
RDGS [114] Eccl 1:2; 2:21-23/ Col 3:1-5,9-11/ Lk 12:13-21

5 - Weekday
Gr RDGS [407] Nm 11:4b-15/ Mt 14:13-21
[*Wh - The Dedication of the Basilica of Saint Mary Major*]
MASS pref I or II of BVM
6 Tue - **The Transfiguration of the Lord (F)**
Wh MASS gl, prop pref
RDGS [614] Dn 7:9-10,13-14/ 2 Pt 1:16-19/ Lk 9:28b-36
7 Wed - Weekday
Gr RDGS [409] Nm 13:1-2,25–14:1,26-29a,34-35/ Mt 15:21-28
[*Rd - St. Sixtus II, Pope, and Companions, Martyrs*]
[*Wh - St. Cajetan, Priest*]
----
* EP = First Vespers (Evening Prayer I) of Holy Father Dominic.
----
8 Thu - **HOLY FATHER DOMINIC, Priest (S)**
Wh MASS gl, *seq*, cr, prop pref
RDGS prop Is 52:7-10 [719.5]/ Ps 96 [721.5]/ 2 Tm 4:1-8 [358]/ Mt 5:13-19 [730.1] or Mt 28:16-20 [724.4] or Lk 10:1-9 [724.8]
9 Fri - Weekday
Gr RDGS [411] Dt 4:32-40/ Mt 16:24-28
[*Rd - St. Teresa Benedicta of the Cross, Virgin and Martyr*]
10 Sat - **St. Lawrence, Deacon and Martyr (F)**
Rd MASS gl, pref I or II of Holy Martyrs
RDGS [618] 2 Cor 9:6-10/ Jn 12:24-26
----
* EP = First Vespers (Evening Prayer I) of the 19th Sunday in Ordinary Time.
=============

11 Sun - **19th Sunday in Ordinary Time** HOURS Week III
Gr MASS gl, cr, pref I-VIII of Sundays in Ordinary Time
RDGS [117] Wis 18:6-9/ Heb 11:1-2,8-19 or 11:1-2,8-12/ Lk 12:32-48 or 12:35-40
12 Mon - Weekday
Gr RDGS [413] Dt 10:12-22/ Mt 17:22-27
[*Wh - St. Jane Frances de Chantal, Religious*]
[*Rd - Bl. Isidore Bakanja, Martyr - Nigeria*]
13 Tue - Weekday
Gr RDGS [414] Dt 31:1-8/ Mt 18:1-5,10, 12-14
[*Rd - SS. Pontian, Pope, and Hippolytus, Priest, Martyrs*]

14 Wed - St. Maximilian Kolbe, Priest and Martyr (M)
Rd RDGS [415] Dt 34:1-12/ Mt 18:15-20

----

* EP = First Vespers (Evening Prayer I) of The Assumption of the Blessed Virgin Mary.

----

15 Thu - **THE ASSUMPTION OF THE BLESSED VIRGIN MARY (S)**
Today is a holy day of obligation in the USA.
Wh MASS gl, cr, prop pref
RDGS Vigil: [621] 1 Chr 15:3-4,15-16; 16:1-2/ 1 Cor 15:54b-57/ Lk 11:27-28
Day: [622] Rv 11:19a; 12:1-6a,10ab/ 1 Cor 15:20-27/ Lk 1:39-56

16 Fri - Weekday
Gr RDGS [417] Jos 24:1-13/ Mt 19:3-12
[*Wh - St. Stephen of Hungary*]

17 Sat - St. Hyacinth of Poland, OP, Priest (M)
Wh RDGS [418] Jos 24:14-29/ Mt 19:13-15
Aa above, or, prop: 1 Thes 2:2b-8 [722.10] or Is 6:1-8 [719.4]/ Ps 117 [721.8]/ Mt 10:7-13 [580]

=============

18 Sun - **20th Sunday in Ordinary Time** HOURS Week IV
Gr MASS gl, cr, pref I-VIII of Sundays in Ordinary Time
RDGS [120] Jer 38:4-6,8-10/ Heb 12:1-4/ Lk 12:49-53

19 Mon -Weekday
Gr RDGS [419] Jgs 2:11-19/ Mt 19:16-22
[*Wh - St. John Eudes, Priest*]

20 Tue - St. Bernard, Abbot and Doctor of the Church (M)
Wh RDGS [420] Jgs 6:11-24a/ Mt 19:23-30

21 Wed - St. Pius X, Pope (M)
Wh RDGS [421] Jgs 9:6-15/ Mt 20:1-16

22 Thu - The Queenship of the Blessed Virgin Mary (M)
Wh MASS pref I or II of BVM
RDGS [422] Jgs 11:29-39a/ Mt 22:1-14

23 Fri - St. Rose (de Flores) of Lima, OP, Virgin (M)
Wh MASS [423] Ru 1:1,3-6,14b-16,22/ Mt 22:34-40
As above, or, prop: 2 Cor 5:14-17 [603] or Sir 3:17-18,20-24 [737.13] or Hos 2:16,17,21-22 [731.2]/ Ps 45 [733.1]/ Jn 15:4-11 [755.12] or Mt 16:24-27 [742.6]

24 Sat - **St. Bartholomew, Apostle (F)**
Rd MASS gl, pref I or II of Apostles
RDGS [629] Rv 21:9b-14/ Jn 1:45-51

----

* EP = First Vespers (Evening Prayer I) of the 21st Sunday in Ordinary Time.

==============

25 Sun - **21st Sunday in Ordinary Time** HOURS Week I
Gr MASS gl, cr, pref I-VIII of Sundays in Ordinary Time
RDGS [123] Is 66:18-21/ Heb 12:5-7,11-13/ Lk 13:22-30

26 Mon - Weekday
Gr RDGS [425] 1 Thes 1:1-5,8b-10/ Mt 23:13-22

27 Tue - St. Monica (M)
Wh RDGS [426] 1 Thes 2:1-8/ Mt 23:23-26

28 Wed - **St. Augustine, Bishop and Doctor of the Church (F)**
Wh MASS gl, pref of Holy Pastors
RDGS prop: Col 3:12-17 [740.11]/ Ps 100/ Jn 17:14-23
Wherever the feastday is celebrated as a solemnity, the first reading is 1 Kgs 3:11-14 [725.1]

29 Thu - The Passion of St. John the Baptist (M)
Rd MASS prop pref
RDGS [428] 1 Thes 3:7-13/ [634] Mk 6:17-29

30 Fri - Weekday
Gr RDGS [429] 1 Thes 4:1-8/ Mt 25:1-13

31 Sat - Weekday
Gr RDGS [430] 1 Thes 4:9-11/ Mt 25:14-30
[*Wh - BVM on Sat or OP Votive Mass*]
MASS pref I or II of BVM
RDGS as above or OP Votive Mass

==============

SEPTEMBER 2019

1 Sun - **22nd Sunday in Ordinary Time** HOURS Week II
Gr MASS gl, cr, pref I-VIII of Sundays in Ordinary Time
RDGS [126] Sir 3:17-18,20,28-29/ Heb 12:18-19,22-24a/ Lk 14:1, 7-14

----

* Today the annual World Day of Prayer for the Care of Creation is observed.

----

2 Mon - Weekday
Gr RDGS [431] 1 Thes 4:13-18/ Lk 4:16-30

[*Labor Day is observed today (National Holiday - USA)*] The following may be used:
Wh *MASS* ***Roman Missal****, Masses and Prayers for Various Needs and Occasions, no. 26 - Mass for the Sanctification of Human Labor*
RDGS ***Lectionary for Mass*** *(vol. IV), For the Holy Church, no.18 - Mass for the Blessing of Human Labor [907-911]*
----
3 Tue - St. Gregory the Great, Pope and Doctor of the Church (M)
Wh RDGS [432] 1 Thes 5:1-6,9-11/ Lk 4:31-37
4 Wed - Weekday
Gr RDGS [433] Col 1:1-8/ Lk 4:38-44
5 Thu - Weekday
Gr RDGS [434] Col 1:9-14/ Lk 5:1-11

OP Today at the Conventual Mass the Anniversary of Deceased Friends and Benefactors is observed.
Wh/Vi/Blk - Anniversary of Deceased Friends and Benefactors
MASS pref I-V for the Dead
RDGS From the Masses for the Dead [1011-1016], especially: 1 Jn 3:1-2 [1014.14]/ Ps 122 [1013.8]/ Mt 25:31-46 [1016.4]
* The liturgy of the hours follows the weekday, not the anniversary.
----
6 Fri - Weekday
Gr RDGS [435] Col 1:15-20/ Lk 5:33-39
7 Sat - Weekday
Gr RDGS [436] Col 1:21-23/ Lk 6:1-5
[*Wh - BVM on Sat or OP Votive Mass*]
MASS pref I or II of BVM
RDGS as above or OP Votive Mass

=============

8 Sun - **23rd Sunday in Ordinary Time** HOURS Week III
Gr MASS gl, cr, pref I-VIII of Sundays in Ordinary Time
RDGS [129] Wis 9:13-18a/ Phlm 9-10,12-17/ Lk 14:25-33
9 Mon - St. Peter Claver, Priest (M) [USA]
Wh RDGS [437] Col 1:24–2:3/ Lk 6:6-11

JW For the Province of St. Joseph the Worker:
9 - Weekday
Gr RDGS [437] Col 1:24–2:3/ Lk 6:6-11
----

10 Tue - Weekday
Gr RDGS [438[Col 2:6-15/ Lk 6:12-19
11 Wed - Weekday
Gr RDGS [439] Col 3:1-11/ Lk 6:20-26
12 Thu - Weekday
Gr RDGS [440] Col 3:12-17/ Lk 6:27-38
[*Wh - The Most Holy Name of Mary*]
MASS pref I or II of BVM
13 Fri - St. John Chrysostom, Bishop and Doctor of the Church (M)
Wh RDGS [441] 1 Tm 1:1-2,12-14/ Lk 6:39-42
14 Sat - **The Exaltation of the Holy Cross (F)**
Rd MASS gl, prop pref or pref I of the Passion of the Lord
RDGS [638] Nm 21:4b-9/ Phil 2:6-11/ Jn 3:13-17

=============

15 Sun - **24th Sunday in Ordinary Time** HOURS Week IV
Gr MASS gl, cr, pref I-VIII of Sundays in Ordinary Time
RDGS [132] Ex 32:7-11,13-14/ 1 Tm 1:12-17/ Lk 15:1-32 or 15:1-10
16 Mon - SS. Cornelius, Pope, and Cyprian, Bishop, Martyrs (M)
Rd RDGS [443] 1 Tm 2:1-8// Lk 7:1-10
17 Tue - Weekday
Gr RDGS [444] 1 Tm 3:1-13/ Lk 7:11-17
[*Wh - St. Robert Bellarmine, Bishop and Doctor of the Church*]
18 Wed - St. Juan Macias, OP, Religious (M)
Wh RDGS [445] 1 Tm 3:14-16/ Lk 7:31-35
As above, or, prop: 1 Kgs 17:8-16 [360] or 1 Jn 3:14-18 [740.16]/ Ps 55 [971.3]/ Mt 6:31-34 [906.1]
19 Thu - Weekday
Gr RDGS [446] 1 Tm 4:12-16/ Lk 7:36-50
[*Rd - St. Januarius, Bishop and Martyr*]
20 Fri - SS. Andrew Kim Tae-gŏn, Priest, and Paul Chŏng Ha-sang, and Companions, Martyrs (M)
Rd RDGS [447] 1 Tm 6:2c-12/ Lk 8:1-3
21 Sat - **St. Matthew, Apostle and Evangelist (F)**
Rd MASS gl, pref I or II of Apostles
RDGS [643] Eph 4:1-7,11-13/ Mt 9:9-13

=============

22 Sun - **25th Sunday in Ordinary Time** HOURS Week I
Gr MASS gl, cr, pref I-VIII of Sundays in Ordinary Time
RDGS [135] Am 8:4-7/ 1 Tm 2:1-8/ Lk 16:1-13 or 16:10-13
23 Mon - St. Pius of Pietrelcina, Priest (M)
Wh RDGS [449] Ezr 1:1-6/ Lk 8:16-18
24 Tue - Weekday
Gr RDGS [450] Ezr 6:7-8,12b,14-20/ Lk 8:19-21
25 Wed - Weekday
Gr RDGS [451] Ezr 9:5-9/ Lk 9:1-6
26 Thu - Weekday
Gr RDGS [452] Hg 1:1-8/ Lk 9:7-9
[*Rd - SS. Cosmas and Damian, Martyrs*]
27 Fri - St. Vincent de Paul, Priest (M)
Wh RDGS [453] Hg 2:1-9/ Lk 9:18-22
28 Sat - SS. Dominic Ibañez de Erquicia, OP, and James Kyushei Tomonaga, OP, Priests, and Lawrence Ruiz of Manila, OP, and Companions, Martyrs in Japan (M)
Rd RDGS [454] Zec 2:5-9,14-15a/ Lk 9:43b-45
As above, or, prop: Rom 8:31-39 [716.2] or Jas 1:2-4,12 [716.7]/ Ps 126 [715.4]/ Lk 9:22-26 [718.4] or Mt 10:17-22 [718.1]

============

29 Sun - **26th Sunday in Ordinary Time** HOURS Week II
Gr MASS gl, cr, pref I-VIII of Sundays in Ordinary Time
RDGS [138] Am 6:1a,4-7/ 1 Tm 6:11-16/ Lk 16:19-31
30 Mon - St. Jerome, Priest and Doctor of the Church (M)
Wh RDGS [455] Zec 8:1-8/ Lk 9:46-50

JW For the Province of St. Joseph the Worker;
* EP = First Vespers (Evening Prayer I) of the Solemnity of Our Lady, Queen of Africa.

OCTOBER 2019

1 Tue - St. Thérèse of the Child Jesus, Virgin and Doctor of the Church (M)
Wh RDGS [456] Zec 8:20-23/ Lk 9:51-56

JW For the Province of St. Joseph the Worker:
1 - **Our Lady, Queen and Patroness of Nigeria (S)**
Wh MASS gl, cr, pref I or II of BVM
RDGS prop Is 55:1-3,6-9/ Eph 2:13-22/ Mt 2:13-15,19-23

----

2 Wed - The Holy Guardian Angels (M)
Wh MASS prop pref
RDGS [457] Neh 2:1-8/ [650] Mt 18:1-5,10
3 Thu - Weekday
Gr RDGS [458] Neh 8:1-4a,5-6,7b-12/ Lk 10:1-12

JW For the Province of St. Joseph the Worker:
3 - St. Thérèse of the Child Jesus, Virgin and Doctor of the Church (M)
Wh RDGS [458] Neh 8:1-4a,5-6,7b-12/ Lk 10:1-12

----

4 Fri - **St. Francis of Assisi (F)**
Wh MASS gl, prop pref
RDGS [651] Sir 50:1b,2-7 or Gal 6:14-18/ /Ps 16/ Mt 11:25-30
5 Sat - Weekday
Gr RDGS [460] Bar 4:5-12,27-29/ Lk 10:17-24
[Wh - Bl. Francis Xavier Seelos, Priest - USA]
[Wh - Bl. Raymond della Vigne of Capua, OP, Priest]
RDGS As above, or, prop: Eph 3:14-19 [740.7]/ Ps 16 [739.3]/ Mk 2:18-22 [311]
[Wh - BVM on Sat or OP Votive Mass]
MASS pref I or II of BVM
RDGS as above or OP Votive Mass

=============

6 Sun - **27th Sunday in Ordinary Time** HOURS Week III
Gr MASS gl, cr, pref I-VIII of Sundays in Ordinary Time
RDGS [141] Hb 1:2-3; 2:2-4/ 2 Tm 1:6-8,13-14/ Lk 17:5-10
7 Mon - **Our Lady of the Rosary (F)**
Wh MASS gl, prop pref or pref I or II of BVM
RDGS prop: Zec 2:14-17 [707.11] or 1 Chr 15:3-4,15-16; 16:1-2 [707.4] or Acts 1:12- 14 [708.1]/ Resp Ps [709.5]/ Lk 1:26-38 [712.4] or Lk 1:39-47 [712.5] or Lk 2:41-51 [712.9]
8 Tue -Weekday
Gr RDGS [462] Jon 3:1-10/ Lk 10:38-42

9 Wed - St. Louis Bertrand, OP, Priest (M)
Wh RDGS [463] Jon 4:1-11/ Lk 11:1-4
As above, or, prop: Gn 12:1-7 [707.2] or Rom 10:9-18 [684]/ Ps 19 [874.1]/ Mk 16:15-18 [519]
10 Thu - Weekday
Gr RDGS [464] Mal 3:13-20b/ Lk 11:5-13

JW 10 - St. Daniel Comboni, Bishop (M)
Wh RDGS [464] Mal 3:13-20b/ Lk 11:5-13

----

11 Fri - Weekday
Gr RDGS [465] Jl 1:13-15; 2:1-2/ Lk 11:15-26
[*Wh - St. John XXIII, Pope*]
12 Sat - Weekday
Gr RDGS [466] Jl 4:12-21/ Lk 11:27-28
[*Wh - BVM on Sat or OP Votive Mass*]
MASS pref I or II of BVM
RDGS as above or OP Votive Mass

=============

13 Sun - **28th Sunday in Ordinary Time** HOURS Week IV
Gr MASS gl, cr, pref I-VIII of Sundays in Ordinary Time
RDGS [144] 2 Kgs 5:14-17/ 2 Tm 2:8-13/ Lk 17:11-19
14 Mon - Weekday
Gr RDGS [467] Rom 1:1-7/ Lk 11:29-32
[*Rd - St. Callistus I, Pope and Martyr*]
15 Tue - St. Teresa of Jesus, Virgin and Doctor of the Church (M)
Wh RDGS [468] Rom 1:16-25/ Lk 11:37-41
16 Wed - Weekday
Gr RDGS [469] Rom 2:1-11/ Lk 11:42-46
[*Wh - St. Hedwig, Religious*]
[*Wh - St. Margaret Mary Alacoque, Virgin*]
17 Thu - St. Ignatius of Antioch, Bishop and Martyr (M)
Rd RDGS [470] Rom 3:21-30/ Lk 11:47-54
18 Fri - **St. Luke, Evangelist (F)**
Rd MASS gl, pref II of Apostles
RDGS [661] 2 Tm 4:10-17b/ Lk 10:1-9
19 Sat - SS. John de Brébeuf and Isaac Jogues, Priests, and Companions, Martyrs (M) [USA]
Rd RDGS [472] Rom 4:13,16-18/ Lk 12:8-12

JW For the Province of St. Joseph the Worker:
19 - Weekday
Gr RDGS [472] Rom 4:13,16-18/ Lk 12:8-12
[*Wh - St. Paul of the Cross, Priest - Nigeria*]
[*Wh - BVM on Sat or OP Votive Mass*]
MASS pref I or II of BVM
RDGS as above or OP Votive Mass

=============

20 Sun - **29th Sunday in Ordinary Time** HOURS Week I
Gr MASS gl, cr, pref I-VIII of Sundays in Ordinary Time
RDGS [147] Ex 17:8-13/ 2 Tm 3:14–4:2/ Lk 18:1-8
21 Mon - Weekday
Gr RDGS [473] Rom 4:20-25/ Lk 12:13-21
22 Tue - Weekday
Gr RDGS [474] Rom 5:12,15b,17-19,20b-21/ Lk 12:35-38
[*Wh - St. John Paul II*]

OP In consecrated churches whose date of consecration is unknown:
- ANNIVERSARY OF THE DEDICATION OF A CONVENTUAL CHURCH (S)
Wh MASS gl, cr, pref I of the Dedication of a Church
RDGS prop Is 56:1,6-7 [701.3])/ Ps 84 [703.3]/ Heb 12:18-19,22-24 [704.3]/ Jn 4:19-24 [706.4]

----

23 Wed - Weekday
Gr RDGS [475] Rom 6:12-18/ Lk 12:39-48
[*Wh - St. John of Capistrano, Priest*]
24 Thu - Weekday
Gr RDGS [476] Rom 6:19-23/ Lk 12:49-53
[*Wh - St. Anthony Mary Claret, Bishop*]
25 Fri - Weekday
Gr RDGS [477] Rom 7:18-25a/ Lk 12:54-59
26 Sat - Weekday
Gr RDGS [478] Rom 8:1-11/ Lk 13:1-9
[*Wh - BVM on Sat or OP Votive Mass*]
MASS pref I or II of BVM
RDGS as above or OP Votive Mass

=============

27 Sun - **30th Sunday in Ordinary Time** HOURS Week II
Gr MASS gl, cr, pref I-VIII of Sundays in Ordinary Time
RDGS [150] Sir 35:12-14,16-18/ 2 Tm 4:6-8,16-18/ Lk 18:9-14

28 Mon - **SS. Simon and Jude, Apostles (F)**
Rd MASS gl, pref I or II of Apostles
RDGS [666] Eph 2:19-22/ Lk 6:12-16
29 Tue - Weekday
Gr RDGS [480] Rom 8:18-25/ Lk 13:18-21
30 Wed - Weekday
Gr RDGS [481] Rom 8:26-30/ Lk 13:22-30
31 Thu - Weekday
Gr RDGS [482] Rom 8:31b-39/ Lk 13:31-35

----

* EP = First Vespers (Evening Prayer I) of All Saints.

NOVEMBER 2019

1 Fri - **ALL SAINTS (S)** Today is a holy day of obligation in the USA
Wh MASS gl, cr, prop pref
RDGS [667] Rv 7:2-4,9-14/ 1 Jn 3:1-3/ Mt 5:1-12a

----

* EP = Second Vespers (Evening Prayer II) of All Saints.

----

2 Sat - **The Commemoration of All the Faithful Departed (All Souls' Day)**
Wh/Vi/Blk MASS pref I-V for the Dead
RDGS [668] Wis 3:1-9/ Rom 5:5-11 or 6:3-9/ Jn 6:37-40
or any readings from no.668 or from the Masses for the Dead [1011-1016]

----

* EP = Vespers (Evening Prayer) for The Commemoration of All the Faithful Departed.

=============

3 Sun - **31st Sunday in Ordinary Time** Hours Week III
Gr MASS gl, cr, pref I-VIII of Sundays in Ordinary Time
RDGS [153] Wis 11:22–12:2/ 2 Thes 1:11–2:2/ Lk 19:1-10
* This year the feastday of St. Martin de Porres, OP, is not observed liturgically.

----

4 Mon - St. Charles Borromeo, Bishop (M)
Wh RDGS [485] Rom 11:29-36/ Lk 14:12-14
5 Tue - Weekday
Gr RDGS [486] Rom 12:5-16b/ Lk 14:15-24

6 Wed - Bl. Alphonsus Navarrete, OP, Priest, and Companions, Martyrs in Japan (M)
Rd RDGS [487] Rom 13:8-10/ Lk 14:25-33
As above, or, prop: Wis 10:17-20 or Acts 20:22-32/ Ps 126 [715.4]/ Jn 15:18-21 [718.6]

JW For the Province of St. Joseph the Worker:
6 - All Saints of Africa (M)
Wh RDGS [487] Rom 13:8-10/ Lk 14:25-33

----

7 Thu - **All Saints of the Order of Preachers (F)**
Wh MASS gl, prop pref or pref I or II of Saints
RDGS prop: Sir 44:1-15 or 2 Cor 6:4-10 [716.4]/ Ps 24 [813.1]/ Mk 10:28-30 [861.3]

8 Thu - Weekday
Gr RDGS [489] Rom 15:14-21/ Lk 16:1-8

OP Today at the Conventual Mass the Anniversary of Deceased Brothers and Sisters of the Order is observed.
Wh/Vi/Blk - Anniversary of Deceased Brothers and Sisters of the Order
MASS pref I-V for the Dead
RDGS From the Masses for the Dead [1011-1016], especially:
Rv 21:1-5a,6b-7 [1012.4]/ Ps 122 [1013.8]/ Jn 17:15-21,24-26

* The liturgy of the hours is taken from the Office for the Dead.

----

9 Sat - **The Dedication of the Lateran Basilica (F)**
Wh MASS gl, pref II of the Dedication of a Church
RDGS [671] Ez 47:1-2,8-9,12/ 1 Cor 3:9c-11,16-17/ Jn 2:13-22

=============

10 Sun - **32nd Sunday in Ordinary Time** HOURS Week IV
Gr MASS gl, cr, pref I-VIII of Sundays in Ordinary Time
RDGS [156] 2 Mc 7:1-2,9-14/ 2 Thes 2:16–3:5/ Lk 20:27-38 or 20:27,34-38

11 Mon - St. Martin of Tours, Bishop (M)
Wh RDGS [491] Wis 1:1-7/ Lk 17:1-6

12 Tue - St. Josaphat, Bishop and Martyr (M)
Rd RDGS [492] Wis 2:23–3:9/ Lk 17:7-10

13 Wed - St. Frances Xavier Cabrini, Virgin (M) [USA]
Wh RDGS [493] Wis 6:1-11/ Lk 17:11-19

JW For the Province of St. Joseph the Worker:
13 - Weekday
Gr RDGS [493] Wis 6:1-11/ Lk 17:11-19

----

14 Thu - Weekday
Gr RDGS [494] Wis 7:22b–8:1/ Lk 17:20-25
15 Fri - **St. Albert the Great, OP, Bishop and Doctor of the Church (F)**
Wh MASS gl, pref of Holy Pastors
RDGS Prop: Sir 6:18-21,33-37 or Jas 3:13-18 [888.3]/ Ps 119 [727.3]/ Mt 25:14-23 [742.12 - short form]

CP Titular Feast of the Central Province: as above.

----

16 Sat - Weekday
Gr RDGS [496] Wis 18:14-16; 19:6-9/ Lk 18:1-8
[*Wh - St. Margaret of Scotland*]
[*Wh - St. Gertrude, virgin*]
[*Wh - BVM on Sat or OP Votive Mass*]
MASS pref I or II of BVM
RDGS as above or OP Votive Mass

=============

17 Sun - **33rd Sunday in Ordinary Time** HOURS Week I
Gr MASS gl, cr, pref I-VIII of Sundays in Ordinary Time
RDGS [159] Mal 3:19-20a/ 2 Thes 3:7-12/ Lk 21:5-19
18 Mon - Weekday
Gr RDGS [497] 1 Mc 1:10-15,41-43,54-57,62-63/ Lk 18:35-43
[*Wh - The Dedication of the Basilicas of SS. Peter and Paul, Apostles*]
MASS pref I or II of Apostles
RDGS [679] Acts 28:11-16,30-31/ Mt 14:22-33
[*Wh - St. Rose Philippine Duchesne, Virgin - USA*]
19 Tue - Weekday
Gr RDGS [498] 2 Mc 6:18-31/ Lk 19:1-10
20 Wed - Weekday
Gr RDGS [499] 2 Mc 7:1,20-31/ Lk 19:11-28
21 Thu - The Presentation of the Blessed Virgin Mary (M)
Wh MASS pref I or II of BVM
RDGS [500] 1 Mc 2:15-29/ Lk 19:41-44
22 Fri - St. Cecilia, Virgin and Martyr (M)
Rd RDGS [501] 1 Mc 4:36-37,52-59/ Lk 19:45-48

23 Sat - Weekday
Gr RDGS [502] 1 Mc 6:1-13/ Lk 20:27-40
[*Rd - St. Clement I, Pope and Martyr*]
[*Wh - St. Columban, Abbot*]
[*Rd - Bl. Miguel Augustín Pro, Priest and Martyr - USA*]
[*Wh - BVM on Sat or OP Votive Mass*]
MASS pref I or II of BVM
RDGS as above or OP Votive Mass

----

* EP = First Vespers (Evening Prayer I) of Our Lord Jesus Christ, King of the Universe.

=============

24 Sun - **OUR LORD JESUS CHRIST, KING OF THE UNIVERSE (S)**
HOURS Week II
Wh MASS gl, cr, prop pref
RDGS [162] 2 Sm 5:1-3/ Col 1:12-20/ Lk 23:35-43

25 Mon - Weekday (34th or Last Week in Ordinary Time)
Gr RDGS [503] Dn 1:1-6,8-20/ Lk 21:1-4
[*Rd - St. Catherine of Alexandria, Virgin and Martyr*]

26 Tue - Weekday
Gr RDGS [504] Dn 2:31-45/ Lk 21:5-11

27 Wed - Weekday
Gr RDGS [505] Dn 5:1-6,13-14,16-17,23-28/ Lk 21:12-19

28 Thu - Weekday
Gr RDGS [506] Dn 6:12-28/ Lk 21:20-28

[*Wh - Thanksgiving Day (National Holiday - USA)*]
MASS Prop Mass and pref for Thanksgiving Day
RDGS Any rdgs from the Mass "In Thanksgiving to God" [943-947], especially: Sir 50:22-24 [943.2]/ 1 Cor 1:3-9 [944.1]/ Lk 17:11- 19 [947.6].

----

29 Fri - Weekday
Gr RDGS [507] Dn 7:2-14/ Lk 21:29-33

30 Sat - **St. Andrew, Apostle (F)**
Rd MASS gl, pref I or II of Apostles
RDGS [684] Rom 10:9-18/ Mt 4:18-22

=============

Prayer Dedicating the Order of Preachers to the Blessed Virgin Mary

Virgin Mother Mary, with trust we approach you. We, your preachers, fly to you who believed in the words sent from heaven and pondered them in your heart. We stand close around you, who are always present to the gathering of apostles.

In you the Word was made flesh, the same Word which we receive, contemplate, praise together, and preach. Therefore, under your guidance we today devote ourselves anew to the ministry of the Word. Furthermore, we declare to you that, hearing with you the Word within ourselves and anointed by the Spirit whose sacred vessel you preeminently are, we are consecrated in the name of Jesus Christ to evangelize the world.

With the eyes of your heart enlightened, you understood the mystery of the Word. Through you we, too, are able to perceive the presence of that same Word in the history of our time, so that we may finally contemplate him face to face.

Through you, the Father sent his Son into the world that he might save it. Through you, we will be powerful in the sight of your people, becoming witnesses of that truth which frees and of that love which unites.

To this place we have brought our needs and here we ponder them. Do you, Mother, give us strength and preserve the harmony of our family, so that what was begun by our profession may be brought to completion by our love for one another, for the salvation of the world, and to the praise and glory of God.

Necrology

for the

U.S. Dominican Provinces of Friars

and the

Province of St. Joseph the Worker

This listing attempts to include all the brethren who have died through September 1, 2018. Any errors or omissions will be corrected if reported to:

Rev. David F. Wright, O.P.
St. Dominic Priory
3005 W. 29th Avenue
Denver, CO 80211
E-mail: wrightop@gmail.com

The letter following each name indicates a brother's Province of affiliation at the time of his death, as follows:

C = Central Province of St. Albert the Great
E = Eastern Province of St. Joseph
N = Nigeria Province of St. Joseph the Worker
S = Southern Province of St. Martin de Porres
W = Western Province of the Most Holy Name

Necrology of the Dominican Friars

? Dominic Raymond Costa ? W

JANUARY

Jan 1 Pius Francis Driscoll 1941 W
John Victor Kane 1991 W
Jacob Bartholomew Joerger 2004 C

Jan 2 Hyacinth Inthout 1861 E
Paul Gerald Corbett 1958 E
Henry Benedict Hughes 1971 E
Richard Raymond King 1979 E
John Francis Dinet 2008 S

Jan 3 Joseph Basil Sheehan 1958 E
James Joseph Regan 1976 C
Daniel Mark Della Penta 1978 C
Albert Hilary Neal 1986 E
Robert Gabriel Quinn 1987 E
William Ferrer Kopfman 1988 E
Daniel Edward Mary Casey 2000 E

Jan 4 Joseph Urban Bergkamp 1971 E
Robert Linus Walker 2016 E

Jan 5 Hyacinth Alfred Meagles 1922 W
Eugene Norbert Brown 1967 E
Dennis Cornelius Kane 1997 E

Jan 6 Patrick Anthony Maher 1952 E
Thomas Benedict Kelly 1971 E
Peter Ralph O'Brien 1971 C
John Luke Lyons 1978 C
John Cyril Fisher 1982 C
Thomas Clement McAndrew 1986 C
Daniel Brendan Crowley 1997 E

Jan 7 John Aloysius Sheil 1941 E
Albion Benedict Morris 1987 W
Richard Vincent Weber 1996 C
Matthias Patrick O'Connor 1998 S
Thomas Bernard Smith 2007 E

Jan 8 John Stephen Moran 1953 E
Luke Joseph Fox 1959 W
Donald Paul Thibault 2017 E

Jan 9 Alexander Mercier 1929 E
James Clement Timony 1930 E
James Raymond Stevenson 1958 C
Joseph Alphonsus Walsh 1963 E
Elwood Ferrer Smith 1992 E
James Stephen Jenner 2003 W
Ralph Theodore Hall 2012 E
Beverly Victor Brown 2017 S

Jan 10 Marian Sanchez 1945 W (Philippines)
John Murphy 1959 E
George Humbert Callan 1971 E
Gordon Frederick Walter 1976 C
William Bertrand Ryan 2004 E

Jan 11 Clarence Gabriel Robert 1935 E
Bernardine Benjamin Myers 1949 C
Bertrand Frederick Clyne 1964 W
John Stephen Peterson 2017 E

Jan 12 Dominic John Donnelly 1960 W
William Aquinas Hinnebusch 1981 E
James Michael Murphy 1992 E

Jan 13 Andrew James Hunt 1929 W
William Augustine Dooley 1981 E
James Brendan Kelly 1998 C
Thomas Richard Heath 2005 E
Emmanuel M. Camilleri 2006 S

more

Jan 13 (continued)
Richard Paul MacLeay 2010 S
David Aloysius Butler 2016 E
George John Dominic Reynolds 2016 C

Jan 14 Hubert Hugo Welsh 1954 E
Robert Louis Rumaggi 1961 E
John Michael Sweeney 1983 E
Felix Gregory Perdigon 1990 W

Jan 15 Milton John Harney 1825 E
Matthew Anthony O'Brien 1871 E
Charles Clement Johnston 1988 S
Vicente M. Peña 2009 S

Jan 16 Paul Luke Sweeney 1938 E

Jan 17 Charles Valerian Reichert 1997 E
Gerard Rouleau Joubert 2004 S
Igba Rumen Vishigh 2000 N
John Thaddeus Murphy 2017 E
Henry B. Groover 2017 S

Jan 18 Timothy Leonard Crowley 1929 E
Reginald John Mitchell 1970 W
George Maurice Robillard 1997 E

Jan 19 Joseph Albert McFadden 1948 E
John Urban Cahill 1971 E
Adolph Dominic Frenay 1971 E
George Gerard Conway 1984 C
Joseph Melchior Wyss 1994 S

Jan 21 Hugh Pius Conly 1904 E
Peter Aloysius Dinahan 1904 E
Hyacinth Joseph Servente 1958 W
Francis Luke Schneider 1976 C
William Raphael Burke 1987 C
Leo Walter Edgar Schnell 1993 E

Jan 22 John Dominic Gubbons 1909 E
Thomas Patrick Gaynor 1969 C
Bernard Giles Waskowski 1970 C
Paul Patrick Walsh 2003 E
Thomas Dominic Kraft 2009 W

Jan 23 James Hyacinth Foster 1941 E
Charles Damian Martineau 1980 E
Walter Lawrence Creahan 1984 E
Walter Brendan Sullivan 1984 E
Joseph Peter Sanguinetti 1997 W
Pierre Hyacinth Conway 2006 E
Russell Jordan Aumann 2007 C

Jan 24 William Reginald Dunn 1911 E
James Andrew Fleming 1967 E
Alphonsus Gustav Braun 1981 W

Jan 25 John Daniel Hickey 1987 S
Joseph Richard Desmond 1996 E
Thomas Quentin Shanley 2002 E
Joseph Martin Connors 2010 E

Jan 26 William Vincent Lanctot 1936 E
Edward Jordan Donovan 1956 E
+ Aloysius Louis Scheerer 1966 E
Joseph Jerome Jurasko 2009 E
Raymond Chrysostom Finn 2016 S
Joseph Charles Fogarty 2016 C

Jan 27 George Justin Rourke 1965 E
Peter Philip Reilly 1992 E
Bernard Kenneth Harkins 2011 E
David Aaron Joseph Coté 2012 E
Edmund Gregory Fay 2012 S
Adrian George Dabash 2017 E

Jan 28 James Louis O'Neill 1904 E
William McClory 1972 W
Victor Humbert Wrobleski 1973 C
Bertrand O'Connor 1992 E
Joseph Peter Kenny 2013 C

Jan 29 Antoninus James Quinn 1961 C
Thomas Hyacinth Sullivan 1966 E
Michael Jordan Minichiello 1969 E
Berchman Hyacinth Scheerer 1978 E
William John Outwater 1979 E

Jan 30 James Corcoran 1878 E
Augustine Bonaventure Sauro 1956 E
Charles Bernardine Carroll 1966 E
Vincent Clement Donovan 1977 E

Jan 31 Benedict John O'Connor 1935 W
John Paulinus Kenny 1992 E
Edward Donald Pikell 1998 C

FEBRUARY

Feb ? Stephen Hyacinth Montgomery 1855 E
\+ John Thomas Hynes 1869 E

Feb 1 Joseph Stanislaus Bernier 1977 C

Feb 2 Charles Pius Welsh 1941 E
William Dean Dooley 1974 W
Alexander Elamah Aleonewese 1992 N
Abraham Thuyen si Ho 1995 S

Feb 3 Joseph Alphonsus Billington 1930 E
Robert Lawrence Lindsay 1969 W
William Leo Duprey 1970 E
Joseph Sylvester Considine 1973 C
Thomas More James McGreevy 2012 W
Robert Philip Ftizsimmons 2013 E

Feb 4
Francis Joseph Dunn 1891 E
Denis Dominic Delaney 1943 E
Bernard Gerald King 1984 E
Thomas Valerian Flynn 1997 C

Feb 5
Grattan Vincent Cleary 1927 E
James Stanislaus Wilburn 1927 E
Richard Simon Trutter 2000 C
Victor Vincent Cavalli 2016 W

Feb 6
+ John Dominic Connolly 1825 E
Dominic Chambers 1894 W
Francis Clement McKenna 1973 E
Eugene Callistus Andres 1978 E
Joseph Anthony Ballard 1986 E
David Arthur O'Connell 1994 E
Ralph Bartholomew Rogawski 2012 S

Feb 7
Thomas Matthew O'Connor 1971 E
Paschal Francis Kelly 1975 C
Benjamin Urban Fay 1977 E
Charles Hugh McKenna 1980 E

Feb 8
Daniel Joseph O'Leary 1835 E
Thomas Dominic Buckman 1855 E
Raymond Sebastian Gillespie 1938 E
George Celestine McGregor 1976 E
William Owen Farrell 1989 S
James Adrian McGee 1993 E

Feb 9
James Dominic Fowler 1930 E
Francis Louis Kelly 1932 E
Francis Dominic McShane 1938 E
Martin Jordan Foley 1945 E
Robert Gregory Lyons 1955 E
Matthew Eugene Cuddy 1963 C
Joseph Reginald Caien 1974 E
Richard Aquinas Stone 1976 E

February

Feb 9
Edward Anselm Vitie 1980 E
Fabian Butler 2003 E
Edward Wayne Conley 2010 S
Lewis Mary William Shea 2010 C

Feb 11 Edward Alphonse Ashfield 1889 E
Basil Edward Kenny 1925 W
Eugene Antoninus Brady 1963 E
James Benedict Heary 1966 E
Joseph Xavier Strenkert 1971 E
John Kusmierz 1984 E
Colum Dennis Daley 1994 N
James Downey John Dominic Campbell 2004 S

Feb 12 John Denis Brackett 1990 E

Feb 13 Timothy Peter O'Rourke 1913 W
Benedict Augustine Blank 1973 W
William Brendan Tarrier 2005 E

Feb 14 Philip Dominic Noon 1859 E
Joseph Thomas Cashin 1896 E
Francis Robert Prout 1988 E
Fabian Richard Larcher 1991 S

Feb 15 James Louis Bertrand Kilkenny 1985 E
Charles Pius Wilson 1992 E
Vincent Ferrer McHenry 2014 E

Feb 16 John Hyacinth Garvey 1882 E
Edward Dominic Donnelly 1920 E
Francis Robert Crowe 2010 C
John Alphonsus Madigan 2011 E

Feb 17 Benedict Thomas Schwertner 1934 E
John Alphonse Fallon 1944 E
Edward Gregory Fitzgerald 1963 E
Henry Athanasius Burke 1965 E
Lawrence Vincent Ferrer Lux 1989 S more

Feb 17 (continued)
Matthew Raymond Scullion 1991 S
William Pius Tefft 1991 E
Osunwoke, Chukwunonye Linus 2018 N
Thomas Paul Leahy 2003 C
Chukwunonye Linus Osunwoke 2018 N

Feb 18 + James Whelan 1878 E
Charles Vincent Metzger 1890 E
Moses Raymond Bloomer 1908 E
Paul Ambrose Bagley 1962 E
Damian Ralph Goggins 1967 C
Francis Ambrose Howley 1970 E
Antonio Moreno 1995 W
Harold Chrysostom Geraets 2001 C
Carlos Vincent Ferrer Griego 2010 C

Feb 19 Raymond John Seamon 1946 W
Charles Matthew Mulvey 1961 E
Francis Daniel Newman 1963 E
John Reginald Dooley 1970 E
Frank Marcolinus Nouza 2015 C
William Kevin Carroll 2017 C

Feb 20 Anthony Dominic Fahy 1871 E (Ireland)
George Augustine Joseph Wilson 1884 E
Carl Sandin 1916 E
Francis Henry Dugan 1941 C
Raymond Nicholas Ashenbrenner 2003 C

Feb 21 + Richard Pius Miles 1860 E
Charles Hyacinth McKenna 1917 E
Clement Augustine Splinter 1923 E
Francis Gerald Keenan 1929 E
Francis Vincent di Michele 1936 E
Humbert Vincent Palmer 1956 W
Gilbert Vincent Ferrer Hartke 1986 E more

Feb. 21 (continued)
Robert Augustine Bordenkircher 2005 S
Brendan Jerome McMullen 2005 C
Robert Urban Sharkey 2009 E
Kurt John Pritzl 2011 E

Feb 22 + Langdon Thomas Grace 1897 E
James Antoninus Rooney 1905 E
Joseph James Mitchell 1939 W
John Lawrence Finnerty 1968 E
Damian Girard Giannotti 1994 W

Feb 23 Samuel Charles Mazzuchelli 1864 E
Simon Thomas Dwyer 1908 W
George Quentin Friel 1974 E
Charles Celestine Rooney 1981 E
Gerald Louis Bertrand Kroeger 2004 C
Winston Benedict M. Ashley 2013 C

Feb 24 William Henrion 1872 E
Joseph Dwyer 1877 E
Raymond Henry Thomas Johns 1902 W
Joseph Aquinas Byrnes 1961 E
Francis Christopher Lehner 1979 E

Feb 25 William John Curran 1965 C
Albert Bertrand Nieser 1987 C
Alfred Anthony Norton 1989 S
John Ephrem Schwind 1993 C
John Malachy Cosgrove 2011 S

Feb 26 Hubert Pius Ralph 1908 E
Arthur Clement Kernan 1911 E
Charles Jerome Callan 1962 E
Francis Louis Kelly 1977 E
Walter Antoninus Ingling 1992 C
Thomas Cajetan Donlan 1999 C
Stephen Terence Chrysler McCabe 2008 W

Feb 27 Daniel Raymond Towle 1936 E
James Gerald Crombie 1964 E
Laurence Frank Krish 1981 C

Feb 28 William Dominic Sullivan 1943 E
Lorenz Pius Johannsen 1957 E
James Louis Mitchell 1957 E
William Athanasius McLoughlin 1977 E
Arthur Lambert McEneaney 1978 E
Arthur Theophane O'Brien 1980 E
Rinaldo Angelico Zarlenga 1986 C (Rome)

Feb 29 Adrian Theodore English 1964 E

MARCH

Mar 1 Francis Joseph Barragan 1945 W
John Raphael O'Connor 1960 E
Francis Nicholas Coughlin 1989 E
Thomas Cornelius Kane 2009 E

Mar 2 James Henry Aerden 1896 W
Thomas Columba McGarry 1988 C
Stephen Thomas Smithers 2007 S
Robert Alan Morris 2015 E

Mar 3 Bernard Patrick Gaynor 1904 W
Robert Patrick Carroll 1967 C
Francis Hugh Scola 1979 E

Mar 4 John Mahoney 1883 E
Antoninus John White 1893 W
John Hyacinth Ford 1911 E
Louis Damian Kennedy 1919 E
Joseph Alphonse Ginet 1934 E
Joseph Stephen McCormack 1967 E
William Augustine Wallace 2015 E

March

Mar 5 Richard Peter O'Rourke 1899 E
Joseph Cyril Coudeyre 1943 E
John Jordan Dwyer 1943 E
James Bernard Kelly 1964 E
Willard Patrick Roney 1988 C
Robert Antoninus Kilbridge 2011 C

Mar 6 Christopher Vincent Lamb 1962 W
Leo Fidelis Boppell 1966 E
James Matthew Erwin 2000 C
Charles Albert Farrell 2010 E
Ralph Valerian Townsend 2011 E

Mar 7 Albert Sadoc Patrick Lawler 1932 W
Clement Albert Drexelius 1981 E
John Dominic Malone 1993 C

Mar 8 Matthew Francis Coyne 1855 E
Ferdinand Gaston Level 1952 E
Henry Ignatius Smith 1957 E
Joachim John Walsh 1962 E

Mar 9 Richard Benedict Montgomery 1840 E
John Dominic Rush 1891 E
Francis Bernard Logan 1922 E
Augustine Louis Naselli 1969 W
Callistus Chimezie Alisiobi 2003 N

Mar 10 Louis Albert Hinnebusch 1958 C
Wenceslaus John Piec 1958 C
Mariner Theodore Smith 1971 E
Joseph Mary Agius 1989 W

Mar 11 Edward Urban Nagle 1965 E
Irving Aloysius Georges 1969 E
Leo Stephen Cannon 1978 E
Walter Hubert Albertson 1985 C

Mar 12 Bernard Mary Connolly 1948 W
Edward Marcellus McGowan 1980 S
John Joseph Snyder 1987 W

Mar 13 George Sylvester Collins 1883 E
Moses Benedict Fortune 1885 E
Vincent George Holl 1955 E
James Raphael Gillis 1979 C
Patrick Luke Thornton 1983 E
Patrick Francis Connolly 2007 E
Ralph Eugene Cahouet 2011 E

Mar 14 James Raymond Ryan 1926 E
Joseph Matthew Stanton 1950 E
Dominic Innocent Donohue 1956 E
John Leonard Curran 1972 C
John Daniel Fearon 1992 W
Robert Bernard O'Riley 2008 C

Mar 15 Francis Michael O'Brien 1871 E
Joseph Reginald Heffernan 1923 E
Charles Vincent Ferrer Fennell 1974 E
Dominic Leo Rothering 2009 C

Mar 16 John Bertrand Kelly 1925 E

Mar 17 Sadoc Francis Vilarassa 1888 W
Cyril Raymond Kane 1930 W
John Dominic Keane 1940 E
George Bernard Hasenfuss 1956 E
Leo Dominic Ross 1988 E

Mar 18 Edward Leo Hughes 1966 C
Michael Alexis Snider 1974 E
Kenneth Cyprian Sullivan 1981 E
Edmund Richard Butler 1988 C
John Peter Gerhard 2005 E
Raymond Ferrer Halligan 2016 E

March

Mar 19 John Thomas Nealis 1864 E
Lawrence Francis Vander Heyden 1960 C
Anthony Figueras 1964 W (Spain)
Dominic Henry Barthelemy 1969 C
Richard Long 1973 E
+ James Michael Dempsey 1996 C

Mar 20 Timothy Martin Rabbitte 1922 E
Joseph Antoninus Heenan 1928 E
Denis Albert Casey 1940 E
John Dominic King 1962 E
Walter Eusebius Heary 1969 E
Clifford Leo Davis 1984 E
Robert Regis O'Connell 1984 E
John Patrick Mulkeen 2000 C

Mar 21 Thomas Dominic Timpane 1929 E
Dominic Innocent Damiani 1932 E
Andrew Patrick Skelly 1938 W
John Thomas McGregor 1968 E
John Andrew Nowlen 1969 E
Francis Charles Duffy 2006 E
Gerald Brian Donovan 2009 S

Mar 22 William Augustine Sullivan 1935 E
James Benedict Hegarty 1943 C
Anthony Donald Kalinowski 1997 C
Edward Quentin Moriarty 2003 C

Mar 23 Thomas Bertrand McCarthy 1986 E

Mar 24 Edward Reginald Craven 1976 E
John Charles Flannery 2013 W
Austin Edward Green 2014 S
David Matthew Hynous 2016 C

Mar 25 James Sylvester Canton 1939 E
Michael Leo Novacki 2000 E

Mar 26 Michael Joseph Eckert 1939 E
Paul Donald McCann 1976 W
John Edward Sullivan 1981 C

Mar 27 Joseph Thomas Jarboe 1887 E
George Alphonse Carr 1898 E
John Paul Egan 1924 E
Paul Edmund Rogers 1975 E
Howard Timothy Sparks 2001 C
Michael Gerard Kyte 2014 C

Mar 28 John Albert Bokel 1902 E
Pius John Murphy 1921 W
Robert Reginald Masterson 1996 S
John James Sullivan 2001 E
James Vincent Nuttall 2009 E-Pakistan
Joseph Daniel Cassidy 2010 E
David Kevin O'Rourke 2012 C

Mar 29 Joseph William Lannen 1935 E
James Celestine McDonough 1967 E
Alexis John Simones 1967 C
Louis Bertrand Boucher 1984 S
John Thomas a'Kempis Eulberg 1984 C
Benedict Albert Rutkauskas 1995 C
John Bonaventure Balsam 2003 S
Edward Mathias Robinson 2012 S

Mar 30 Patrick Louis Lynch 1886 E
William Thomas Purchase 1953 E
Matthew Burke 1971 C
James Wilfrid Matthew Regan 2000 C
George Leonard Cochran 2013 E

Mar 31 Timothy Victor Dwyer 1983 E
Eric de Wasseige 2010 C (Belgium)

APRIL

Apr 1 Harold Camillus Boyd 1969 E
Joseph Fabian Beever 1972 E
Harry Arthur Hall 1974 C
James Hilary Mulcahy 1974 E
Richard Brendan Connolly 1977 C
Thomas Aquinas Morrison 2014 C

Apr 2 Joseph Augustine Sheuerman 1862 E
Thomas Dominic Chang 1967 E
John Fabian Whittaker 1997 E

Apr 3 Paul Victor Flanagan 1942 E
Richard Jerome Meaney 1946 E
Bernard Charles Murray 1946 C
Francis Leonard Grady 1959 E
Maurice Daniel Nelan 1992 E
Joseph Bede McGroarty 2007 E

Apr 4 Louis Gerald Clark 1945 W
Gabriel Mary Aloysius Knauff 1962 W
Walter Dominic Clifford 1971 E
Stephen Kieran Smith 2018 S

Apr 5 Thomas Sylvester McGovern 1921 E
Leo Peter Craig 1951 E
Francis Leibold 2007 E
Terence Stephen McDermott 1963 E

Apr 6 Aloysius Alfred Sibila 1975 E
William Leo Patten 1992 E
Leo Arthur Kinsella 2008 C

Apr 7 Thomas Hyacinth Justa 1911 E
Edward Damian Grady 1969 E
Thomas Damian Smith 1988 C
Thomas Dominic Rover 1998 E
Alfred Augustine Gately 2000 E

Apr 8 Franklin Chrysostom Seery 1943 C
John Stanislaus Kennedy 1962 E
Louis James Robinson 1970 W
Walter Hubert Horan 1983 E
Edward Paul Farrell 1989 E
Robert Louis Every 2000 S

Apr 9 Charles Pius Montgomery 1860 E
William Glennon 1863 E
John Ambrose McHugh 1950 E
Daniel Michael Galliher 1961 E
Vincent Ferrer Leo Kienberger 1963 C
Joseph Basil Boyd 1989 E
Thomas Vincent DiFede 2011 E

Apr 10 Francis James Marion 1888 W
Arthur Vincent Higgins 1917 E
Anthony Patrick O'Keefe 1917 W
Ignatius Schranz 1959 C
Andrew James Winters 1980 S
Peter Van To Mai 2008 S
Clement Daniel Tyulen 2014 N

Apr 11 Lawrence Thomas Breen 1907 W
Joseph Henry Slinger 1909 E
Daniel Joseph Kennedy 1930 E
Joseph Raymond Vivier 1958 E
John Bertrand Fitzgerald 1981 E (Ireland)
Lawrence Edward Banfield 2011 W
Thomas Paul Chrysostom Raftery 2018 W

Apr 12 Edward Lawrence Van Becelaere 1946 C
Timothy Joachim Murphy 1965 E
Richard Edward Vahey 1987 E
Edward Paul Doyle 1997 E
Joseph Innocent Hren 2009 C

Apr 13 George William Roach 1955 C
William Jerome Olson 1956 E
John Dominic Kearney 1989 E

April

Apr 14 + Joseph Sadoc Alemany 1888 E/W
Sebastian John Owens 1946 W
Orville Theodore Carl 1991 E
Frederick Michael Jelly 2000 E
Salvatore Joseph Rossetti 2007 E
Francis Raymond Mullin 2009 E
Paul Joseph Philibert 2016 S

Apr 15 Michael Lombard 1869 E
John Charles Traynor 1879 W
Edmond John Harrington 1908 W
William Reginald Mahoney 1935 E
Ambrose Wilhelm Jura 1973 C
Vitoldus Thomas Ziuraitis 1990 E
Robert Henry Lavigne 2001 W

Apr 16 Thomas Augustine Scallon 1885 E
Gregory James Moore 2016 C

Apr 17 Francis John Hornick 1888 W
Thomas Dennis Gilligan 1981 E
John Pius Sullivan 1998 E

Apr 18 Charles Leo Gainor 1967 C
Frederick Eugene Klueg 1988 C

Apr 19 Jordan Eugene Caldwell 1879 W
John Sylvester Fraher 1944 C
Robert William Feehan 1963 W
Frederick Alan Milmore 1982 E
Bernard George Hart 1993 E
Francis Hyacinth Maguire 2006 E

Apr 20 Thomas Fidelis Conlon 1959 E
Francis Emmanuel Yonkus 1980 E
James Linus Dolan 2018 S-Peru

Apr 21 Charles Walter Sadlier 1977 E

Apr 22 + John Timothy McNicholas 1950 E
John Alphonsus Turzick 1979 E
Damian Callery Fandal 1994 S
James Raymond Motl 2016 C

Apr 23 Harold Regis Barron 2000 E
Bertrand Alan Gobeille 2002 C

Apr 24 James Alphonse Sheridan 1889 E
Kieran James Holden 1907 E
Arthur Charles O'Neil 1920 E
Henry John Dominic Van den Wildenberg 1921 E
John Berchmans Affleck 1955 E
Raymond Eugene Kavanah 1955 C
Robert Joseph Slavin 1961 E
Leo Martin Shea 1972 C
William Augustine Carroll 1988 E
Lucius M. Weber 1989 S
Salvatore Di Nardo 2004 W

Apr 25 Paul Vignot Barrett 1993 S

Apr 26 John Bonaventure O'Connor 1926 E
William Charles Kelly 1944 E
Leo Anthony Hofstee 1986 W

Apr 27 Patrick Redmond 1873 E
Roscoe Francis Larpenteur 1947 C
John Beckett 1957 W
Francis Jerome Barth 1969 C
Philip Louis Bertrand Hanley 1982 E
Anthony Henry Denier 2004 C

Apr 28 Reginald James Newell 1932 W
Edward Sylvester McGinnis 1935 E
Joseph Celestine Taylor 1982 E
William Andrew Newman 2009 E

Apr 29 John Hyacinth O'Connell 1892 E
John Thomas Mulvin 1947 E
George Brendan Connaughton 1961 E
Paul Arthur Bernardin 2002 E

Apr 30 Thomas Shields 1878 E
Maurice Felix Beale 1924 E
William Thomas Lewis 1978 W
William Antoninus Walsh 1981 E
Joseph Edmund Bidwill 2018 C

MAY

May 1 Michael Thomas McNicholas 1947 E
Alexius John Driscoll 1967 C
Albert Stephen Moraczewski 2008 S
John Janko Zagar 2013 W

May 2 Thomas Antoninus Osbourne 1859 E
Patrick Francis Murphy 1909 E
Raphael Joseph Corcoran 1936 W
William Bonaventure Murphy 1982 C
Hugh Hilary McGinley 1990 E

May 3 Michael James Joyce 1864 E
Joseph Damian Pendergast 1942 E
Arthur John McKeon 1965 W
William Peter Elder 1984 S
Robert Eric Bond 2004 E

May 4 James Alphonse Daly 1914 E
Francis Paul Spalding 1959 E

May 5 Thomas Humbert Dailey 1972 C
William Hyacinth Brenda 2008 S
Richard Norbert Buckley 2016 E

May 6 William Thomas Willet 1824 E
Bernard Alphonse Brady 1881 E
Peter Clement Coll 1887 E
Francis Andrew O'Neil 1909 E

May 7 Joseph Henry Schroeder 1942 C
John Antoninus Baverso 1950 E
Ralph Marcolinus Rascher 1980 E
William Jordan O'Donnell 1995 E
James Richard McAvey 2001 E

May 8 Arthur Lawrence McMahon 1952 E
Francis Jordan Fanning 1955 E
Joseph Barnabas Briggs 1972 E
Thomas Fabian Carey 1972 E
John Dominic Walsh 1982 E
Michael Edward Stock 1996 E

May 9 Edward Joseph O'Toole 1958 E
Francis Norbert Wendell 1970 E

May 10 Thomas Martin 1859 E
Frederick Francis Feeley 1925 E
Hyacinth Lawrence Martin 1940 E

May 11 Charles Gabriel Moore 1949 E
Charles Fidelis Christmas 1960 E
John Francis Henry McDonnell 1988 C

May 12 John Antoninus Keheeley 1902 E

May 13 Charles Clement McGonagle 1960 E
John William Bernacki 2018 C

May 14 Francis Madden 1892 E
George Mark Scanlon 1937 E
John Patrick Reid 1985 E

May 15 Augustine Adolph Durkin 1938 E
Alfred Peter Bachand 1976 E
Gerard Eugene Halloran 1988 C

May

May 16 Patrick Francis Corley 1919 E
Sylvester Raphael Brockbank 1937 E

May 17 John James Murphy 1975 E
Robert Regis Hovald 2003 C

May 18 James Henry Barry 1931 E
Thomas Michael Barrett 1935 W (Ireland)
William Joseph O'Leary 1941 E
George Thomas Kinsella 1959 C
Quitman Francis Beckley 1963 E
Christopher Raymond Fritter 1985 W

May 19 Salvator Emmanuel Anastasi 1915 E
Ambrose Lamarre 1940 W (Canada)
Conrad Robert Antonsen 1993 W
Victor Samuel LaMotte 1999 C

May 20 Patrick Feeney 1895 E
John Philip Archdeacon 1941 E
Lawrence Ambrose Smith 1945 E
Jeremiah Thomas Fitzgerald 1950 E
Joseph Louis Pastorelli 1952 E
Camillus Edward Lillie 1966 C
Patrick Pius Heasley 1968 E
Peter Francis Nash 1968 E
Raymond Peter Nuttall 1968 E
James Joachim Pender 1969 C

May 21 James Dominic Kearney 1894 E
John Berchmans Logan 1953 E
Alexander Stephen Connelly 1968 E
John Raymond Grace 1980 E
Barnabas William Curtin 1987 W
Joseph Reginald Herlihy 1989 E
William Robert Barron 1994 S

May 22 Maurice Peter Powers 1890 E
Victor Gordon White 1960 W (England)
Isidore V. Vicente 2017 S

May 23 Samuel Thomas Wilson 1824 E
Thomas Leo Halloran 1950 W
Austin Charles Sheehan 1968 E
John Augustine Myhan 1992 W

May 24 Ernest Albert Hogan 1979 E

May 25 William Raymond Tuite 1833 E
Julius Martin Mattingly 1991 E
Matthew Flavian Morry 2008 E

May 26 John Bernard Mulgrew 1991 E
Cyril Walter Burke 1997 E
Harold Dana Ostdiek 2009 C
Richard Norbert Buckley 2016 E

May 27 Albert Reinhart 1913 E
Daniel Antoninus Wynn 1949 C
John Edward O'Hearn 1970 E
Randolf Bertrand Johannsen 1973 E
Joseph Leo Kelly 1981 S

May 28 Claudius Martin Blake 1942 W
Thomas Luke Weiland 1960 E
+ James Charles Burke 1994 E

May 29 Joseph Thomas Murphy 1893 E
John Edmund Marr 1992 C

May 30William Quinn 1919 E
Thomas a'Kempis Reilly 1957 C
Thomas Carl Gabisch 1969 W
John Joachim Bauer 1979 E
Norbert D. Fihn 1994 W

May 31 Dominic McGrane 1862 E
Dennis Dominic Crowley 1887 E
James Luke Devine 1947 E
Edward Lawrence Skelly 1966 E
Walter Angelus Murtaugh 1983 E
Leroy Gilbert Hensley 2014 C

JUNE

Jun 1 Charles Dominic Bowling 1866 E
Richard George Ferris 1952 E
Michael Thomas McNicholas 1968 C
Thomas Aquinas Clifford 2011 S

Jun 2 Michael Connell 1902 E
Leo John Haggerty 1928 W
Matthew Earl Hanley 1972 E
Michael O'Hara 1974 W
Kevin Cornelius Thissen 2005 C

Jun 3 Damian Joseph O'Brien 1931 W
Froyland Casquero 1950 W (Spain)
David Fidelis Anderson 1973 E
Raymond Ambrose Cevasco 1983 E
Paul Robert Starrs 1984 W
John Ferrer Arnold 2003 E

Jun 4 Bernard Aloysius McLaughlin 1953 E
William Richard Clark 1957 E
Harold Adrian Wade 1989 E
Raymond Smith 1990 E
Gilbert Donald Sherry 1990 C
Blaise William Schauer 1996 W
Gerald Bertrand Morahan 1998 C

Jun 5 Henry Chrysostom Graham 1966 E
Joseph Paul Gruber 1967 E
Emmanuel Louis Nugent 1968 C
Peter Valerian Manning 1989 E

Jun 6 Michael Joachim Kennedy 1925 E
Matthew Leo Carolan 1938 E
David Gregory O'Connor 1949 E
Henry Paul Cunningham 1961 E
Hubert Francis Ward 1983 W
Francis Stephen Redmond 1984 S
William John Dominic Logan 2012 S

Jun 7 Octave Damian Parent 1969 E
William Linus Up de Graff 1985 S
John Camillus Rubba 2000 E
John Raymond Corr 2005 S
Joseph Urban Goss 2006 S

Jun 8 Michael Paul O'Sullivan 1920 E
Joseph Clement Nowlen 1941 E
William Justin Dillon 1978 E
Paschal Francis Hunt 1983 C
Avelino Gonzalez Baragano 1992 S (Spain)

Jun 9 Anthony Raymond Gangloff 1864 E
Lawrence Flaherty 1890 E
Gregory Raphael Scholz 1946 C
Dionysius Joseph Mueller 1962 W
Frederick Damien Hoesli 2015 E

Jun 10 William Humbert Kane 1970 C
Gabriel Robert Lane 1974 C
Thomas Bernard Feucht 1980 W

Jun 11 William Justin Aldridge 2005 S

Jun 12 Francis Aloysius Spencer 1913 E
Victor Francis O'Daniel 1960 E
Austin Ralph Powell 2001 C
Norman Hilarion Fenton 2011 E

Jun 13 Leo Arthur Arnoult 1982 S
John Jordan Reichert 1987 E
Vincent Italo Zarlenga 2010 C

Jun 14 Louis Michael O'Brien 1939 E
Arthur Basil Coté 1944 C
Antoninus Albert Healy 1959 W
Peter John Houlihan 1968 C
Matthew Raymond Lord 1969 W
Joseph Sebastian Angers 1978 C
Mark Maurice Barron 1982 S
Richard Raymond Francis Shaw 1990 C

June

Jun 15 James Mark Egan 1966 E
Roderick Malachy Dooley 2002 C

Jun 16 Michael Martin Boughan 1879 E
Leonard Joseph Lockingen 1911 E
Hugh Joseph McManus 1937 E
Francis John Twohig 1945 E
Francis Dominic Alwaise 1947 E
James Walter Hackett 1978 E
Antoninus Lawrence Hall 1981 W
James Stanislaus McHatton 1997 S
Louis Bertrand Osbourne 2016 E

Jun 17 Patrick Shepherd 1860 E
Louis John Daniel 1896 W
James William Owens 1969 E
Robert Edward Brennan 1975 E
Francisco V. Vicente 2017 W
Joseph Christopher Johnson 2017 E

Jun 18 Edward Joachim Cummings 1931 E
Lawrence Edward Jagoe 1951 W
John Felix Ryan 1964 E
William Raymond Dillon 1974 E
Fabian Stan Parmisano 2009 W

Jun 19 + Richard Luke Concanen 1810 E (Ireland)
Patrick John Callaghan 1904 W

Jun 20 George Innocent Smith 1950 E
Gilbert James Graham 2008 C

Jun 21 Martin Stanislaus Welsh 1961 E
Thomas Edward Dominic Hennessey 1993 E
John Dominic Tamburello 2006 S
Gerald Thaddeus Coverdale 2008 S
Joseph Luke Lennon 2011 E
Kenneth Archibold France-Kelly 2015 E

Jun 22 Augustine Peter Walker 1900 E
James Patrick Heaney 1904 E

Jun 23 Joseph Cyprian Brady 1929 E
James Bertrand Bailey 1954 E
Lawrence Richard Dolan 1964 E

Jun 24 Francis Edward Dominic Fenwick 1973 E
Martin Edward Dominic Garry 1973 E

Jun 25 Edward Leo Spence 1949 E
Joseph Martin Connors 2010 E

Jun 27 Philip Dennis Brady 1973 C
William Dalmatius Marrin 1982 E
William Terence O'Shaughnessy 1998 E

Jun 28 Lorenzo Cornelius McCarthy 1941 E
Peter Alexis Casterot 1952 E
James Gerald Joyce 1979 E
James Terence Sullivan 2001 E

Jun 29 Reginald Thomas Hickey 1888 W
Arthur Hyacinth Chandler 1945 E
Daniel John Francis Connell 1971 C
Joseph Maurice Sherer 1996 E
Nicholas Francis Halligan 1997 E
Albert John-Marie Coburn 2001 S
Thomas Chrysostom McVey 2009 E

Jun 30 John Albert McShane 1882 E
William Antoninus Marchant 1938 E
Joseph Richard Clark 1952 E

JULY

Jul 1 John Jerome Durkin 1950 E
John Paul McDermott 1957 E
Paul Michael James 1990 E

Jul 2 Patrick Simon Gough 1863 E
Vincent Francis Vinyes 1892 W
Mannes Bernard Doogan 1912 W
Robert Reginald Maguire 1961 E
John Alfred Sullivan 1972 E
Joseph Aloysius McTigue 1981 E
Fred Valerian LaFrance 2011 E

July

Jul 3 James Vincent Daly 1881 E
Sylvester Ambrose Pendergast 1888 E
Edward Kevin Gallagher 1941 C
Marcellus John Nugent 1972 C
James Bonaventure Zusy 2004 C
Jerome Joachim Haladus 2008 E

Jul 4 Henry Augustine Brewer 1900 E
Joseph Edward Kernan 1928 E
Dominic William Noon 1952 C
Paul Charles McKenna 1990 E

Jul 5 William Ignatius Ricarby 1901 E
Cyril Andrew Geary 1977 C
James Bernard Walker 1984 C
Robert Ceslaus Prazan 1998 C
Thomas Clark Alexander Moore 2009 C

Jul 6 John Vincent Corrigan 1916 E
Francis Xavier O'Neil 1940 E
Theodore Clement Mary Thuente 1960 E
John Justin Madrick 1980 S
Charles Bonaventure Crowley 1995 E

Jul 7 Constantius Louis Egan 1899 E
Vincent James Martin 1967 E
Ferdinand Norbert Georges 1969 E
Joseph Adrian Manning 1972 E
Mark Douglas McPhee 1994 W
John Paul Mahoney 1996 E

Jul 8 Dominic Joseph Lentz 1883 W
Simon Eugene Brady 1886 E
James Martin Fahey 1916 W
Owen Edmund Rocks 1966 E
James Anselm McCabe 1982 E
Jude Dawson-Amoah 2009 N

Jul 9 William Martin O'Rourke 1912 E
James Albert O'Brien 1933 E
Crocian Ignatius Cappellino 1952 E
Walter Pius Alger 1984 E
Thomas Clement Nagle 1993 E
Jude Thaddeus Dawson-Amoah 2009 N

Jul 10 James Bernard Geraghty 1860 E
Patrick Thomas Faunt 1886 E
Joseph Bernard Hughes 1944 E
Leo Louis Farrell 1953 E
Anthony Henry Suso Hamel 1991 S
William Gannon 2016 E

Jul 11 James Dominic Keating 2005 E
Edward Elms Everitt 2011 S

Jul 12 Joseph Bernard Kircher 1939 E
John Hyacinth Kaszczuk 1940 E
Raymond Leo Lewis 1969 W

Jul 13 George Bonaventure Paulis 1956 E
Francis Norbert Reynolds 1972 E

Jul 14 John George Albert Alleman 1865 E
Francis Cubero 1883 E
Gerald Lawrence Vann 1963 W (England)
Robert Patrick Sullivan 1969 E
Michael Andrew Kavanaugh 1974 C
Ronald Angelus Stanley 2012 E
Andrew Cyril Fabian 2017 C

Jul 15 Edward Joseph Farmer 1920 E
Robert Francis Conway 1994 E
Michael Morris 2016 W
Martin Michael Downey 2017 E

July

Jul 16 John Dominic Kelly 1937 E
Anthony Bucci 1965 E
Willard Paul Doane 1969 E
Edward Lawrence Hunt 1980 E
Charles Raymond Alger 1984 E
Sean Brendan Doherty 1996 W
George Michael Matanic 2013 W
Robert Damian Myett 2018 E

Jul 17 Thomas Patrick Dowd 1957 E
Edward Timothy Quinlan 1964 E
Philip J. Lamberty 2008 S

Jul 18 Raphael Muñoz 1830 E
Joseph John Sullivan 1960 E
Colin Vincent McEachen 1993 W
Wilfred Gabriel Hoff 2014 C

Jul 19 Peter Daniel Cronin 1894 W
Augustine Ignatius Walsh 1908 E
Raphael John Kelleher 1961 C
Francis Joseph Walsh 1961 W
John Joseph Ryan 1998 E
Robert Regis Heuschkel 2017 E

Jul 20 Eugene Bernard Farley 1923 E
John Phillips 1923 E
George Ignatius Conlan 1926 E
Colman Bonaventure Morrison 1973 E
Robert Francis Bailey 1984 E
John Brendan Larnen 1992 E
James Bernard Sheriden 1998 E
Richard Bontempo 2016 S

Jul 21 John Sylvester Collins 1884 E
Joseph Christopher Pino 1958 E
Raphael Monaghan 1966 C
Aloysius O'Bierne 1975 E
Edward Berchmans Finnin 1991 E
Edward Jude Ferrick 1994 E
John Gerald McGreevy 2016 C

Jul 22 Raymond Jerome Dewdney 1972 E
Iltud Evans 1972 W (England)
Anthony Ambrose Kroutch 1980 W
Richard Edward Krukonis 1995 E

Jul 23 Martin Peter Clancy 1879 E
James Dominic Hoban 1891 E
Felix Velez 1943 W (Spain)
John Aloysius Jordan 1946 E
John Charles Norton 2009 S

Jul 24 Nicholas Raymond Young 1876 E
Joseph Vincent Dailey 1972 E
Walter Jerome Tierney 1978 E
Thomas Damian Sheehan 2000 S
Robert Ignatius Campbell 2002 C
Martin Francis McCormick 2008 C
Arthur Joseph Payne 2011 E

Jul 25 Dennis Ambrose McNamara 1969 C
Bernard Gabriel Schneider 1972 E
Philip Fabian Mulhern 1984 E
Stephen John Dominic Skalko 2000 E

Jul 26 John Henry Healy 1963 E
James Cleophas Connolly 1973 E

Jul 27 Constantius Edward Warren 1923 W
Timothy Albert O'Connor 1960 E
Michael Luke McCaffrey 1981 E
Robert Joachim Miller 2005 C
John Robert Dolehide 2012 C

Jul 28 John Patrick McNerney 1952 E
George Hyacinth Kopfman 1972 E
John James Lonergan 1980 E
Kevin Edmund Carr 1986 W
James Joseph Davis 2011 E

Jul 29 Thomas Joachim Smith 1974 E
Paul Francis William Cronin 1981 E
Alan Eugene Smith 1985 E
William David Moriarty 1990 E
Paul Ogbogu Odey 1996 N

Jul 30 Edward Matthias Heffernan 1974 E
James Luke McKenney 1974 E
John Norbert Morgenthaler 2004 S
John Jerome Conroy 2005 E

Jul 31 John Ambrose Durkin 1885 E
James Paul Devereaux 1889 E
Paul Thomas Henry 1919 W
Antoninus Francis Fox 1954 C
Vincent Marcellus Raetz 1983 E
Christopher Hugo Moschini 2001 W

AUGUST

Aug 1 Adelard Benedict Dionne 1982 E
David Paul Frusti 1991 C

Aug 2 Eugene Vincent Flood 1917 E
Frederick Francis Breit 1938 E
John Paul Roach 1940 E
Mark James Rooden 1945 W
Pius Edward Harris 1978 W
David Adam Balla 1979 C
Godwin Okwesili 2005 N
Lawrence L. Pandolfo 2009 S
Daniel Thaddeus Davies 2018 E

Aug 3 Francis Joseph Thomas Cady 1900 E
Francis Gabriel Horn 1943 E
Gregory Harry Anderson 2004 W
Charles Henry Santoro 2004 C

Aug 4 James Aloysius O'Dwyer 1896 E
Joseph Sebastian O'Connell 1956 E
Martin Ambrose McDermott 1971 C
Dominic Urban Corigliano 1980 E
Robert Vincent Foerstler 2006 W
Paul Akagan-Ketch 2013 N
Thomas Declan McGonigle 2015 C

Aug 5 Ambrose Lindsey 1890 E
Richard Hyacinth Goggin 1898 E
Patrick Vincent Hartigan 1904 E
Paul Augustine Skehan 1954 E
Lloyd Albert Mahler 1995 E
Robert Bede Jagoe 2014 C
Jordan Anthony McGrath 2018 C

Aug 6 Robert Dennis Zusy 2000 C

Aug 7 Joseph Augustine Kelly 1885 E
John Hyacinth Lynch 1908 E
Edward Augustine Martin 1946 E
James Martin Murphy 1956 E
Charles Augustine Haverty 1971 E
Richard Ambrose Fleck 2009 E

Aug 8 Francis Xavier Finnegan 1968 E
William Cyprian Cenkner 2003 S

Aug 9 James Timothy Wrinn 2006 S

Aug 10 Dennis Joseph Meagher 1896 E
Bruno Hyacinth Kowalkowski 1998 C

August

Aug 11 Bernard Antoninus Enis 1938 E
Edward Constantius La More 1958 E
Edward Eugene Holohan 1976 E
Martin Keith Hopkins 1980 C
James Timothy Carney 1995 E (Pakistan)
Joseph Benjamin Russell 2014 C

Aug 12 Michael Leahy 1909 E
John Aloysius Hinch 1941 E
Edmund Barnabas Leary 1977 E
Cletus John Wessels 2009 C

Aug 13 Raymond Stephen McGonagle 1963 E
Vincent Anthony Guagliardo 1995 W
Harvey Bartholomew Schaller 1998 E

Aug 14 Malachy Donlon 1951 E
Paul Adrian Elnen 1956 E
George Dominic Morris 1982 E
Matthew Francis Chen 1996 E

Aug 15 William Raymond Lawler 1964 C
Peter Patrick Miles 1984 W
Timothy Louis Bertrand Curry 1990 S
Joseph Hilary Kenny 1995 E
William Dominic Brady 1999 S
Gerald Albert Buckley 2017 W

Aug 16 Simon Patrick Devereaux 1864 E
Alfred Quentin Lister 1997 S
John Patrick McGovern 2005 E

Aug 17 Frederick Clement Foley 1955 E
Andrew John Henry 1971 C
Terence Albert Holachek 2005 S

Aug 18 Robert Gabriel Turbitt 1924 E
Reginald John Rabadan 1967 C (Croatia)
Nicholas Robert Reid 1996 E
Richard Robert Farmer 2006 C

Aug 19 Stephen Alexander McEachern 1989 W
Robert Ferrer Pieper 1998 C

Aug 20 John Ceslaus Fenwick 1815 E
Michael Dominic Lilly 1901 E
James Gerard O'Donnell 1949 E
Michael Quentin Goldrick 1972 E
John Gerard Curley 1982 E
Paul Gerard Hinnebusch 2002 S
George Lawrence Concordia 2015 E

Aug 21 Leo Lawrence Bernard 1965 E
Thomas Gregory Mullaney 1973 E
James Ambrose Fitzpatrick 1978 E
Bernard Patrick Condon 1986 W
James Cajetan Sheehan 1997 E

Aug 22 Louis Marie Daigle 1954 C
Bernard Charles Arnheim 1989 W
Leon Mancinelli 2001 E
Thomas Malachy Cumiskey 2002 S

Aug 23 James Christopher Gunning 1971 E
John Isidore Roberts 1971 E
Edward Louis Martin 2000 E
Bartholomew Paul Fu 2001 E
William David Folsey 2018 E

Aug 24 Walter Charles Durbin 1961 E
Edward Leonard Phillips 1967 E
Charles Raphael Hess 1998 W
James Muller 2017 E

Aug 25 James Hyacinth Clarkson 1849 E
Vincent Edward Simpson 1934 E
Antoninus Regis Lewis 1938 W
Dominic Frederick Perry 1939 E
William Lawrence Costello 1956 E
William Alphonse Fincel 1972 E

August

Aug 26 Luke Andrew Kelly 1972 W
John Luke Barnes 1989 E
William Pius Conlan 2000 S
Denis M. Swann 2005 E
Gary Benedict Baer 2012 C

Aug 27 Michael Antoninus McFeely 1908 E
Joseph Thomas Keelty 1916 E
James Francis Colbert 1931 E
William Gregory Cummins 1954 E
John Thomas Murray 1975 E
John Gerald Masterson 1993 S
Ronald Hector Henry 2012 S

Aug 28 Martin Albert Sheehan 1929 E
Francis Bartholomew Campbell 1930 E
John Victor Williams 1963 E
Edward Aquinas McDermott 1981 E
Joseph Clement Della Penta 1999 C
Jerome Aquinas O'Leary 2002 C
Paul Okello Nygawir 2002 E

Aug 29 John Albert Bokel 1878 E
John Raymond McGarvey 1878 E
Peter Thomas McAllister 1944 E
Owen Ignatius Beatty 1963 E

Aug 30 Francis Dominic Connolly 1972 E
Gino Eugene Bondi 1994 E
Henry Joseph Hoppe 1994 S
Terence John Reilly 2016 W

Aug 31 David John Staszak 1998 C
Joseph Cletus Kiefer 2012 W

SEPTEMBER

Sep 1 Francis Theodore Quinn 1916 E
John Vincent Fitzgerald 1967 E
Anthony William Rennar 1992 E
Matthew Vincent Reilly 1999 E

Sep 2 Augustine William Netterville 1954 W
Roland Jerome McCann 1976 E
Christopher Gerald Kiesling 1986 C

Sep 3 John Augustine Hill 1828 E
James Gaffney 1895 E
William Peter McIntyre 1942 C
Thomas Matthew McGlynn 1977 E

Sep 4 John Michael Barrett 1965 E

Sep 5 Edward Pius De Cantillon 1900 E

Sep 6 James Reginald Coffey 1985 E

Sep 7 George Boniface Stratemeier 1947 E
Mark Paul Geary 1997 S
John Thaddeus Carrigan 2009 E

Sep 8 Vincent Regis Whalen 1952 C
Richard Hugh Wreisner 2001 C

Sep 9 Thomas Raymond Fallon 1875 E
Leo Urban Cull 1946 E
Thomas Hugh McBrien 1988 E
Urban Francis Bates 2003 W
John Anthony McMahon 2011 E

Sep 10 Julius Chibuzor Nwaibc 2014 N

Sep 11 Bernard Hanlon 1890 E
Francis Justin Routh 1955 E
John Francis McCadden 1959 E
Charles Edmund Hayes 1968 C
Hyacinth Peter Frendo 1996 E (Rome)

September

Sep 12 Allen Thomas Blake 1942 E
Walter Gregory Moran 1956 E
John Justin Costello 1964 E
Louis Maurice O'Leary 1974 E
John Matthew Donahue 1982 E
James Raphael Comeau 1983 S

Sep 13 Patrick Thomas Barry 1891 E
Florent Gutierrez-Martin 1973 W (H. Rosary)
Thomas Ceslaus McGowan 1996 E

Sep 14 Patrick Joseph Corcoran 1936 E
Michael Augustine O'Connor 1957 E
Conrad Donald Cassidy 1994 C
Joseph Hugh Mulhern 2008 E

Sep 15 James Thomas à Kempis McKenna 1965 E
Herman Martin Killian 1968 E
Thomas Timothy Shea 1980 E
Bernard Constantius Werner 1985 E

Sep 16 Robert Joseph Huggins 1877 E
Arthur Ralph McCaffrey 1964 E
James Dalmatius Enright 1970 E
William Raymond Bonniwell 1984 E

Sep 17 James Vincent Bullock 1851 E
John Raymond Cleary 1855 E
John James Magee 1868 E
Stephen John Rice 1934 W
Joseph Fidelis Gilsenan 1987 E
John Santoro 1995 E
Charles Reginald Malatesta 2001 C

Sep 18 Dominic Hyacinth Noon 1894 E
Henry Francis Cooper 1928 E
Joseph John Welsh 1948 E
Patrick James Conaty 1979 E
Robert Raymond Blais 2011 E

Sep 19 Patrick Joseph Scannell 1878 E
Frederick Aquinas Gordon 1974 E
John Jordan Duffy 1975 E
Charles John Dominic Corcoran 1984 C

Sep 21 James Benedict McGovern 1918 E
Leo Matthew Heagen 1951 E
Thomas Kevin Connolly 1975 E
Paul Natale Zammit 1995 W

Sep 22 Anthony Gerald McCabe 1965 E
Walter James Conway 1972 C
Stuart Bede Campbell 1986 E
Mark Gorski 2016 W

Sep 23 George Raymond Dailey 1873 E
Martin Edward Allen 1936 E
Adam Paul Curran 1953 E
Joseph Bernard Malvey 1977 C
William David Folsey 2018 E

Sep 24 John Dominic James Kavanaugh 1948 C
Francis Louis Bertrand Cunningham 1963 C
John Malachy Smith 1963 E
Bernard Paschal Shaffer 1965 E
Francis Louis Bertrand O'Connell 1969 E

Sep 25 Joseph Gerard Precourt 1968 E
John Walter Caverly 1991 S
Stephen Vatroslav Budrovich 1994 C (Croatia)
Charles Sebastian Jorn 2002 E
Daniel Jerome Kennedy 2002 E
Joseph Clement Burns 2014 E

Sep 26 + Edward Dominic Fenwick 1832 E
Emile Dalmatius Reville 1879 E (France)
Damien Marie Saintourens 1920 (Canada)
Cyprian Edward McDonnell 1935 W
Hyacinth Joseph Valine 1992 W more

Sep 26 (continued)
Gregory Joseph Going 2000 S
Vincent-Mary Joseph Akpala 2010 N
Anthony Gilbert Cordeiro 2010 W

Sep 27 Gregory Joseph Rourke 1943 W
Aloysius Basil Begley 1978 E
Edward Justin Brodie 1985 E

Sep 28 William Peter Hutton 1853 E
Humbert Henry Kelly 1954 W
Richard Donald Danilowicz 1980 E

Sep 29 John Morrin 1843 E
Martin Patrick Cassin 1892 W
Bertrand Valentine Martin 1933 W

Sep 30 Michael Whelan 1884 E
John Samuel Jones 1905 W
Arthur Pius McEvoy 1964 E
Stephen G. Goetz 1989 S

OCTOBER

Oct 1 Daniel Alexander Rocks 1922 E
John Pius O'Brien 1993 S
James Justin Cunnigham 1996 E

Oct 2 Daniel Peter Coughlin 1940 E
James Andrew O'Donnell 1947 C
John Donald McMahon 1962 E
Philip Cyprian Skehan 1970 E
John Anthony Foley 1976 E
William Aquinas Norton 1978 W

Oct 3 John Brendan Reese 1970 E
Edward Henry Schmidt 1985 E
Edward Sylvester Dorsey 1990 E
Patrick Michael James Clancy 2001 C

Oct 4 Dominic M. Kneip 1877 E
Hugh John Leonard 1930 E
Wilfred Robert Mulvey 1967 C
Clement Matthew Breen 1989 C
Samuel Raymond Parsons 2011 W

Oct 5 John Antoninus Rochford 1896 E
Francis Aloysius Ryan 1897 E
Daniel Flavian Reilly 1962 E
Edward Hyacinth Putz 1984 E
Bernard Christopher McCabe 2004 E

Oct 6 Paul Doyle 1881 E
Jeremiah Pius Turner 1892 E
Henry Vincent Wild 1959 E
James Joachim M. Thiel 2004 C
James Colum Burke 2009 S
Bernard Lawrence Keitz 2011 E
Norman Haddad 2016 E

Oct 7 Bartholomew Vincent Carey 1873 E
Patrick Vincent Keogh 1896 E
John Aquinas Cowan 1947 E
Raymond Bernard St. George 1977 E
Edward Boniface Halton 1983 E
Paul Leo Slanina 1987 E
Carson Fabian Champlin 1989 C

Oct 8 Joseph Francis Harris 1957 C
William Leo Whalen 1957 E
Gerard William Ehler 1999 W
Raymond Thomas Aquinas Collins 2000 E
Peter Ambrose Windbacher 2001 N

Oct 9 Dennis Augustine O'Brien 1873 E
Albert Basil Davidson 1954 E
Mark Charles Verschure 1956 C
Michael Peter Coyne 1967 E
John Anselm Egan 1988 S
Edward Sebastian Carlson 1990 C
Loren M. Pelick 2009 S
Aaron Hilario Arce 2012 S

October

Oct 10 Thomas Horace McElhatton 1965 W
John Joseph McInnis 1968 E

Oct 11 John Fidelis Spalding 1999 E

Oct 12 Martin Joseph Jordan 1962 E
George Gregory Herold 1974 E
Adolph Isnard Van Erkel 1990 E (Flanders)
William Joseph Hill 2001 E

Oct 13 + William Dominic O'Carroll 1880 E (Ireland)
Sadoc Francis Welch 1912 W
John Clement Gilroy 1935 E
Bertrand James Connolly 1964 C
Joseph John Angers 2001 S
Miguel Crescentio Gonzalez 1978 W (Holy Rosary)

Oct 14 José Leonardo Vázquez Pavón 1997 S
Anthony Antoninus Jurgelaitis 2000 E
Ernest Francis Kelly 2002 E
Lawrence Gerard (Kenneth) Farrell 2012 W

Oct 15 Henry Arthur Kelly 1976 E
Hugh Justin McManus 1979 E
Lawrence Edward Sanguinetti 1985 W
Robert Jerome Botthof 2014 C

Oct 16 Patrick McKenna 1852 E
William Mannes O'Beirne 1996 E
James Vincent Watson 2010 E
Roderick Marvin Brown 2013 C

Oct 17 John Dominic Sheehy 1873 E
James Paul Aldridge 1941 E
Stanislaus William McDermott 1945 W

Oct 18 Ambrose Francis Wilson 1911 W
Emmanuel Aloysius Hughes 1918 E
Dennis Patrick Kane 1964 W
Arthur Cornelius Tierney 1968 E

Oct 19 William Francis O'Connor 1932 E
John Theodore Finnegan 1937 E
James Raymond Meagher 1954 E
John Bernard Walsh 1968 E
Andrew Anthony Bujnak 1970 E
John Reginald Smith 1971 E
Victor Francis A. Celio 2010 S
John Aquinas Powers 2010 S
Jesús de Vianney Guerra 2014 S

Oct 20 Thomas Louis Power 1906 E
William Andrew Goetz 1918 E
Charles John O'Connell 1955 E
Philip Bennett Pendis 1961 C
William Reginald Neu 2016 C

Oct 21 Thomas Augustine Dyson 1898 W

Oct 22 Anthony John McGovern 1932 E
John Aloysius Segren 1979 E
John Leonard Callahan 1984 C
Daniel Lambert Shannon 1989 E
Thomas Reginald Peterson 2000 E
Joseph Humbert Determan 2016 S

Oct 23 Stephen Alphonse Gavin 1943 E
Gerald Mark O'Dowd 1964 E
Albert Mark Schratz 1996 E (Pakistan)

Oct 24 Alphonsus Peter Riley 1932 W
John Hugh Hartnett 1963 E
Walter John Heath 1987 E
John Joseph Mahoney 1990 E

Oct 25 Andrew Michael Whelan 1953 E
Hugh Gregory McBride 1964 E
Vincent Edward Connell 1972 E
Edward Vincent Ferrer Clancy 1973 E
Stan Edward Gorski 1978 C
Jeremiah Michael Burmeister 1989 W

Oct 26 John Benedict McLaughlin 1869 E

Oct 27 John Jordan Warnock 1955 E
Peter Carrol Curran 1982 W
Thomas Matthias Cain 2000 S

Oct 28 Patrick Dominic Mullahy 1937 E

Oct 29 Francis Hyacinth Eterovich 1981 C (Croatia)
Paul Ferrer Ryan 1999 C
John Charles Fabian 2014 C
John Jude Locchetto 2014 E

Oct 30 Reginald Vincent Hughes 1965 C
Anselm M. Thomas Townsend 1977 C
Joseph George Forquer 1990 C
Edward Martin McDonald 1995 E

Oct 31 Andrew Francis Pope 1943 W
John Joseph Molloy 1961 E
Joseph Bertrand Soeldner 1991 E
Frank Currier Quinn 2008 C

NOVEMBER

Nov 1 James Raymond Meagher 1889 E
Eligius Suarez-Fernandez 1962 W (Mexico)
Paul Christopher Perrotta 1969 E
Joseph Innocent Reardon 1977 C

Nov 2 Peter Pitt 1861 E
Eugene William Holland 1926 E
Patrick Benedict Doyle 1935 E
Jerome Timothy Treacy 1973 C

Nov 3 Peter Hyacinth Doherty 1861 E
William Antoninus Horgan 1886 E
Raphael George Carpentier 1967 C
Charles Alphonsus Carosella 1985 S
Hilary Justin Freeman 1998 C

more

Nov 3 (continued)
John Gerard O'Connell 2001 C
Joseph D. Konkel 2013 S
Jerome Matthias Walsh 2013 C

Nov 4 Ralph Augustine La Plante 1921 E
Duane Anthony Brown 1997 C
Alphonsus Philip Smith 2007 E
Francis Kevin O'Connell 2008 E

Nov 5 John Theodore Van den Broek 1851 E (Germany)
Louis Andrew Berenguer 1856 W
James John McLarney 1969 E

Nov 6 Patrick Joseph Doherty 1895 E
John Philip Vallely 1930 E
Rudolph Francis Vollmer 1971 E

Nov 7 James Bailey 1944 C
Justin James Butler 1973 W
James Aloysius Driscoll 2013 E

Nov 8 Anthony George Perry 1876 W
Thomas Aquinas Patrick Fitzsimmons 1896 W
William Raymond McNicholas 1987 S
James Cornelius Hahn 2008 C

Nov 9 Stanislaus Edward Olsen 1962 W
Bruno Casimir Zvirblis 1972 E
James Arthur McInerney 1980 C
Gerald Jude Pidcock 2003 C

Nov 10 Daniel Walter van Rooy 1985 C

Nov 11 Stephen Bernard Jurasko 1986 E

Nov 12 Ferdinand Ramos Y Gomez Perez 1962 W (Mexico)
Henry Francis Hohman 1963 C
Charles Provenzale 1972 E
Joseph Eugene Madden 1977 E more

Nov 12 (continued)
Gerard Walter Martin 1981 W
Warren Bede Dennis 1993 S
Paul Chrysostom Curran 1995 E
Francis Dominic Nealy 1999 E

Nov 13 James Andrew Mackin 1938 E
Felix Francis Cassidy 2015 W

Nov 14 Joseph James Baverso 1956 E
Kevin Albert Wall 1988 W
John Joseph Klaia 2003 W

Nov 15 Chrysostom Joseph McDonald 1953 C
Daniel John Ward 1966 W
John Francis Monroe 1971 E
Thomas Chrysostom Donnelly 1973 E
Mark Paul Francis Small 1986 E
Joseph Louis Asturias 1995 W
Michael Joseph McGovern 2017 C

Nov 16 Martin Pius Spalding 1892 E
John Barnabas Davis 2017 E

Nov 17 Jude Raymond Nogar 1967 C
William Humbert Crilly 1969 C
William Cyprian Meehan 1971 E
Leonard Edward Curtis 1995 S
Alan Augustine Evans 1999 E

Nov 18 James Vincent Edelen 1892 E
Jeremiah Clement O'Mahoney 1911 E
Richard Vernon Walker 1944 E
Charles Ignatius Litzinger 1966 E
William Richard Byrnes 1978 C
John Jordan Lacey 1988 E
Cornelius Philip Forster 1993 E
Leo Byron Thomas 1997 W
Charles Henry O'Brien 2014 E

Nov 19 Albert Benedict Thomas 1989 E
Malcom Sylvester Willoughby 2015 E
Paul Edward Scanlon 2015 W

Nov 20 Robert Antoninus Angier 1850 E
John Ambrose Dempsey 1929 E
Walter Gabriel Scanlon 1950 E
John Bernard Schneider 1971 C
George Cajetan Reilly 1972 E
Charles Valerian Lucier 1997 E
Edward Henry Gallagher 2009 E

Nov 21 William Charles Daley 1936 E
John Peter Morrissey 1960 E
William Ferrer Cassidy 1974 E
Camillus Albert Musselman 1983 E
William Regis Ryan 1992 E
Michael Dominick McGreal 1998 C
Edward Louis Cleary 2011 C
Harold John Baptist Gerlach 2013 C

Nov 22 John Justin Kennedy 1951 E
John Ignatius Reardon 2004 S
Raymond Martin McCabe 2005 E
Edmund John Way 2008 E
Raymond Charles Bertheaux 2011 W
Valentine Ambrose McInnes 2011 S

Nov 23 Stephen Byrne 1887 E
Louis Casenave 1893 E
Gerard Edward McMullan 1950 W
Walter Raphael Farrell 1951 C
+ Edward Celestine Daly 1964 E
Joseph Ignatius McGuiness 1994 E

Nov 24 John Butler 1919 E
Cyril Aloysius Therres 1962 C
James Cajetan Chereso 1980 C
Thomas Leonard Fallon 1993 E
Louis Luke Turon 2013 E
Richard Martin Patrick 2015 S

Nov 25 Thomas Joseph Ryan 1877 E
William Francis Linahan 1917 E
Lawrence Francis Kearney 1924 E
John Peter Farrell 2003 E
Bede Francis Eugene Wilks 2011 W

Nov 26 Samuel Louis Montgomery 1863 E
John Clement Kent 1907 E
Ivan Innocent Maria Bojanic 1980 C
Andrew James Sloan 1984 W

Nov 27 Peter Augustine Anderson 1850 E
John Anthony Reddy 1919 E
Eugene Aloysius Wilson 1939 E
Joseph Thomas Aquinas Joyce 1967 E
Nicholas Hugh Serror 1972 E
Thomas Lawrence Kearney 2010 C
Nadra John Benedict Joseph 2011 E

Nov 28 Nicholas Dominic Young 1878 E
Joseph Reginald Higgins 1939 E
Richard Mannes McDermott 1957 E
John Stanley Gaines 1981 C

Nov 29 Michael Joseph Ripple 1938 E
James Ferrer McManus 1975 E
Joseph Eugene Hyde 1983 E
John Raymond Gore 1984 W

Nov 30 Michael Norbert Connell 1957 E
John Stanislaus Dillon 1995 E
Bernard George Nintemann 1996 C

DECEMBER

Dec ? Maurice James Egan ? E
Robert Young 1812 E
J. Mulholland 1845-48 E
D. Moran 1845-48 E

more

Dec ? (continued)
Thomas Lawrence Keenan 1845-48 E
John Dominic Urquhart 1856-57 E
Hyacinth Doherty 1860-61 E
Joseph Poelking 1866 E

Dec 1 Louis Reginald Bertrand 1926 E
Richard John Thomas Ford 1937 E
Andrew Dominic Glynn 1942 C
John Jordan Dillon 1944 E
William Anthony O'Connell 1945 E
Stephen Eugene Murray 1952 C
William George Mottey 1960 E

Dec 2 Francis Augustine Gaffney 1922 E
James Moneta Moyna 2005 E
John Linus Sullivan 2011 E

Dec 3 William Dempflin 1912 W
Hugh Francis Lilly 1914 E
Sebastian Maurice Bohan 1928 W
Philip Edward Emmans 1957 C
William Joseph McLaughlin 1958 E
David Joseph Donovan 1971 E
Mark R. Leuer 1992 S

Dec 4 Thomas Tully 1901 E
Mannes Urbanc 1965 C
Edmund Ceslaus McEniry 1977 E
Daniel Patrick Brady 2001 S
Richard Mark Heath 2005 E
John Fabian Cunningham 2006 E

Dec 5 James Clement Kearney 1960 E
Antoninus Edmund Baxter 1961 C
Joseph Michael Reilly 1975 E
Angel Vizcarra 2004 S

December

Dec 6 Patrick John Barry 1935 W
Stephen Thomas Connelly 1965 W
Dominic Francis Hoffman 1998 W

Dec 7 Michael Antoninus Horrigan 1907 E
Raymond Cajetan Cervera 1911 W
Walter Philip Thamm 1941 E
Arthur Cornelius Richmeier 1986 C
Robert Justin Hennessey 2003 E

Dec 8 Phillip Carroll 1902 W
Charles Robert Auth 1995 E
Thomas Finbar Carroll 1998 E
Walter Vargas Soleto 2003 C

Dec 9 Michael Benedict Flynn 1925 E
Martin Augustine Waldron 1926 E
Matthew Leo Osbourn 1961 E
Charles Dennis 1995 W

Dec 10 Thomas Edward O'Neill 1903 W
James Bartholomew McGwin 1940 E
Thomas Raphael Gallagher 1979 E
Clement Eugene Collins 1995 S

Dec 11 John Henry O'Callahan 1967 E
Joseph Bertrand Taylor 1979 E
Patrick Leo LaBelle 2017 W

Dec 12 Eugene Charles Monckton 1959 C
Joseph John Fulton 1998 W

Dec 13 Hilary Regis Ahern 1954 E
Frederick Jordan Baeszler 1955 E
Sydney James Cyril Osbourn 1969 E
Charles Bernardine Quirk 1972 E
Vincent Harold Champine 2007 C

Dec 14 Vincent Dominic Dolan 1959 E
Eduardo Ponciano Zelaya Sanchez 1976 C
Vincent Cyril Dore 1984 E
Paul Julius Adamchak 1994 E
+ Thomas Cajetan Kelly 2011 E

Dec 15 Matthew Francis McGrath 1870 E
Charles Mannes Delavigne 1969 E
James Raymond Maloney 1974 E
John Joseph Stephen Reidy 1977 C
Victor Sylvester Feltrop 1984 C
Edwin Ignatius Masterson 1984 E
Bernard David Kenny 1995 E

Dec 16 Sydney Albert Clarkson 1901 E
Dominic John Maher 1950 W
William Bertrand Mahoney 1980 C
Patrick John Kelly 1983 W
Thomas William Martin 1995 S

Dec 17 John Pius Moran 1912 E
John Edward Keefer 2008 S
James Stephen Murray 2014 E

Dec 18 Robert Ignatius Tucker 1971 C
Peter James West 1979 C
Thomas Urban Mullaney 1989 E

Dec 19 Richard Pius Cahill 1937 E
+ Thaddeus Edward Lawton 1966 C
Daniel Louis Carter 1978 C
Carl James Breitfeller 1991 E
Robert Donald Reilly 1992 E
Giles Alfred Klapperich 2015 C
Robert Alexius Goedert 2015 C
Robert William Vaughn 2016 E

Dec 20 Albert Thomas Muller 1966 W
John James McDonald 1996 C
John Finnbarr Hayes 2017 W

December

Dec 21 Thomas Henry 1917 E
Ambrose Paschal Regan 1957 E
John Nicholas Walsh 1982 S
Paul John Dominic Scanlon 1996 E

Dec 22 John Vincent Reisdorf 1891 E
Bartholomew Edward Ryan 1964 C
Martin David Burke 1973 E
Thomas Hilary Kaufman 1995 E
Francis Leo Regan 1995 E
Thomas Marcellus Coskren 2003 E

Dec 23 James Benedict Hallisy 1867 E
James Bernard Spearing 1904 E
John Anthony Murtaugh 1947 C
Bernard John Dering 1960 C
Glenn Kocchi 1967 C
Andrew Richard McQuillan 1971 E
Martin Lloyd Hartung 1990 C

Dec 24 Thomas Anthony Hickey 1914 E
Vincent Raymond Burnell 1958 E

Dec 25 Thomas James Polin 1838 E
Francis Bertrand Gorman 1948 E
Frederick Cornelius Hickey 1966 E
Lewis Anthony Springman 1992 E
John Patrick McGuire 2016 E

Dec 26 William Louis Mary Downes 1983 E
Charles Thomas Shannon 1998 E

Dec 27 Edgar Regis Landy 1947 E
John Wilfred Ryan 1980 W
Thomas Arnold Morrison 1989 E
John Edmund O'Connell 1994 S
Joseph Filadelfio Romero 2003 W
George Gerard Maley 2009 E

December

Dec 28 John Hyacinth McGrady 1838 E
Alvarus Emmanuel Joseph 1942 W
Michael Anselm Murray 1957 E
Herman Damian Schneider 1963 E
Chester Adrian Myers 1968 C
Robert Dennis Riley 2006 E

Dec 29 James Reginald Kennedy 1929 E
Joseph Joachim Hagan 1986 C

Dec 30 Hyacinth James Derham 1891 W
Ceslaus Thomas Clancy 1948 W
Sylvester Clyde Chamberlain 1957 W
John Richard Clarke 1980 C
James Athansius Weisheipl 1984 C
Francis Hyacinth Roth 1985 C
Daniel Dalmatius Madden 2004 S

Dec 31 Sebastian Henry Shaw 1918 W
Philip Daniel Purtill 1955 W
Benjamin Aquinas Arend 1976 C
Paul Kevin Meagher 1976 W
Richard Thomas Aquinas Murphy 1998 S

Alphabetic Necrology of the Dominican Friars

Adamchak,	Paul Julius	1994	Dec 14	E
Aerden,	James Henry	1896	Mar 2	W
Affleck,	John Berchmans	1955	Apr 24	E
Agius,	Joseph Mary	1989	Mar 10	W
Ahern,	Hilary Regis	1954	Dec 13	E
Akagan-Ketch,	Paul	2013	Aug 4	Nigeria
Akpala,	Vincent-Mary Joseph	2010	Sep 26	Nigeria
Albertson,	Walter Hubert	1985	Mar 11	C
Aldridge,	1. James Paul	1941	Oct 17	E
	2. William Justin	2005	Jun 11	S
Alemany,	+ Joseph Sadoc	1888	Apr 14	E
Aleonewese,	Alexander Elamah	1992	Feb 2	Nigeria
Alger,	1. Charles Raymond	1984	Jul 16	E
	2. Walter Pius	1984	Jul 9	E
Alisiobi,	Callistus Chimezie	2003	Mar 9	Nigeria
Alleman,	John George Albert	1865	Jul 14	E
Allen,	Martin Edward	1936	Sep 23	E
Alwaise,	Francis Dominic	1947	Jun 16	E
Anastasi,	Salvator Emmanuel	1915	May 19	E
Anderson,	1. David Fidelis	1973	Jun 3	E
	2. Gregory Harry	2004	Aug 3	W
	3. Peter Augustine	1850	Nov 27	E
Andres,	Eugene Callistus	1978	Feb 6	E
Angers,	1. John Joseph	2001	Oct 13	S
	2. Joseph Sebastian	1978	Jun 14	C
Angier,	Robert Antoninus	1850	Nov 20	E
Antonsen,	Conrad Robert	1993	May 19	W
Arce,	Aaron Hilario	2012	Oct 9	S
Archdeacon,	John Philip	1941	May 20	E
Arend,	Benjamin Aquinas	1976	Dec 31	C
Arnheim,	Bernard Charles	1989	Aug 22	W
Arnold,	John Ferrer	2003	June 3	E
Arnoult,	Leo Arthur	1982	Jun 13	S
Ashenbrenner,	Raymond Nicholas	2003	Feb 20	C
Ashfield,	Edward Alphonse	1889	Feb 11	E
Ashley,	Winston Benedict M.	2013	Feb 23	C
Asturias,	Joseph Louis	1995	Nov 15	W
Aumann,	Russell Jordan	2007	Jan 23	C
Auth,	Charles Robert	1995	Dec 8	E

Bachand,	Alfred Peter	1976	May 15	E
Baer,	Gary Benedict	2012	Aug 26	C
Baeszler,	Frederick Jordan	1955	Dec 13	E
Bagley,	Paul Ambrose	1962	Feb 18	E
Bailey,	1. James	1944	Nov 7	C
	2. James Bertrand	1954	Jun 23	E
	3. Robert Francis	1984	Jul 20	E
Balla,	David Adam	1979	Aug 2	C
Ballard,	Joseph Anthony	1986	Feb 6	E
Balsam,	John Bonaventure	2003	Mar 29	S
Banfield,	Lawrence Edward	2011	Apr 11	W
Barnes,	John Luke	1989	Aug 26	E
Barragan,	Francis Joseph	1945	Mar 1	W
Barrett,	1. John Michael	1965	Sep 4	E
	2. Paul Vignot	1993	Apr 25	S
	3. Thomas Michael	1935	May 18	W (Ireland)
Barron,	1. Harold Regis	2000	Apr 23	E
	2. Mark Maurice	1982	Jun 14	S
	3. William Robert	1994	May 21	S
Barry,	1. James Henry	1931	May 18	E
	2. Patrick John	1935	Dec 6	W
	3. Patrick Thomas	1891	Sep 13	E
Barth,	Francis Jerome	1969	Apr 27	C
Barthelemy,	Dominic Henry	1969	Mar 19	C
Bates,	Urban Francis	2003	Sep 9	W
Bauer,	John Joachim	1979	May 30	E
Baverso,	1. John Antoninus	1950	May 7	E
	2. Joseph James	1956	Nov 14	E
Baxter,	Antoninus Edmund	1961	Dec 5	C
Beale,	Maurice Felix	1924	Apr 30	E
Beatty,	Owen Ignatius	1963	Aug 29	E
Beckett,	John	1957	Apr 27	W
Beckley,	Quitman Francis	1963	May 18	E
Beever,	Joseph Fabian	1972	Apr 1	E
Begley,	Aloysius Basil	1978	Sep 27	E
Berenguer,	Louis Andrew	1856	Nov 5	W
Bergkamp,	Joseph Urban	1971	Jan 4	E
Bernacki,	John William	2018	May 13	C
Bernard,	Leo Lawrence	1965	Aug 21	E
Bernardin,	Paul Arthur	2002	Apr 29	E
Bernier,	Joseph Stanislaus	1977	Feb 1	C
Bertheaux,	Raymond Charles	2011	Nov 22	W
Bertrand,	Louis Reginald	1926	Dec 1	E
Bidwill,	Joseph Edmund	2018	Apr 30	C

Billington,	Joseph Alphonsus	1930	Feb 3	E
Blais,	Robert Raymond	2011	Sep 18	E
Blake,	1. Allen Thomas	1942	Sep 12	E
	2. Claudius Martin	1942	May 28	W
Blank,	Benedict Augustine	1973	Feb 13	W
Bloomer,	Moses Raymond	1908	Feb 18	E
Bohan,	Sebastian Maurice	1928	Dec 3	W
Bojanic,	Ivan Innocent Maria	1980	Nov 26	C
Bokel,	1. John Albert	1878	Aug 29	E
	2. John Albert	1902	Mar 28	E
Bond,	Robert Eric	2004	May 3	E
Bondi,	Gino Eugene	1994	Aug 30	E
Bonniwell,	William Raymond	1984	Sep 16	E
Bontempo,	Richard J.	2016	Jul 20	S
Boppell,	Leo Fidelis	1966	Mar 6	E
Bordenkircher,	Robert Augustine	2005	Feb 21	S
Botthof,	Robert Jerome	2014	Oct 15	C
Boucher,	Louis Bertrand	1984	Mar 29	S
Boughan,	Michael Martin	1879	Jun 16	E
Bowling,	Charles Dominic	1866	Jun 1	E
Boyd,	1. Harold Camillus	1969	Apr 1	E
	2. Joseph Basil	1989	Apr 9	E
Brackett,	John Denis	1990	Feb 12	E
Brady,	1. Bernard Alphonse	1881	May 6	E
	2. Daniel Patrick	2001	Dec 4	S
	3. Eugene Antoninus	1963	Feb 11	E
	4. Joseph Cyprian	1929	Jun 23	E
	5. Philip Dennis	1973	Jun 27	C
	6. Simon Eugene	1886	Jul 8	E
	7. William Dominic	1999	Aug 15	S
Braun,	Alphonsus Gustav	1981	Jan 24	W
Breen,	1. Clement Matthew	1989	Oct 4	C
	2. Lawrence Thomas	1907	Apr 11	W
Breit,	Frederick Francis	1938	Aug 2	E
Breitfeller,	Carl James	1991	Dec 19	E
Brenda,	William Hyacinth	2008	May 5	S
Brennan,	Robert Edward	1975	Jun 17	E
Brewer,	Henry Augustine	1900	Jul 4	E
Briggs,	Joseph Barnabas	1972	May 8	E
Brockbank,	Sylvester Raphael	1937	May 16	E
Brodie,	Edward Justin	1985	Sep 27	E
Brown,	1. Beverly Victor	2017	Jan 9	S
	2. Duane Anthony	1997	Nov 4	C
	3. Eugene Norbert	1967	Jan 5	E

	4. Roderick Marvin	2013	Oct 16	C
Bucci,	Anthony	1965	Jul 16	E
Buckley,	1. Gerald Albert	2017	Aug 15	E
	2. Richard Norbert	2016	May 26	E
Buckman,	Thomas Dominic	1855	Feb 8	E
Budrovich,	Stephen Vatroslav	1994	Sep 25	C (Croatia)
Bujnak,	Andrew Anthony	1970	Oct 19	E
Bullock,	James Vincent	1851	Sep 17	E
Burke,	1. Cyril Walter	1997	May 26	E
	2. Henry Athanasius	1965	Feb 17	E
	3. + James Charles	1994	May 28	E
	4. James Colum	2009	Oct 6	S
	5. Martin David	1973	Dec 22	E
	6. Matthew	1971	Mar 30	C
	7. William Raphael	1987	Jan 21	C
Burmeister,	Jeremiah Michael	1989	Oct 25	W
Burnell,	Vincent Raymond	1958	Dec 24	E
Burns,	Joseph Clement	2014	Sep 25	E
Butler,	1. David Aloysius	2016	Jan 13	E
	2. Edmund Richard	1988	Mar 18	C
	3. Fabian	2003	Feb 9	E
	4. John	1919	Nov 24	E
	5. Justin James	1973	Nov 7	W
Byrne,	Stephen	1887	Nov 23	E
Byrnes,	1. Joseph Aquinas	1961	Feb 24	E
	2. William Richard	1978	Nov 18	C
Cady,	Francis Joseph Thomas	1900	Aug 3	E
Cahill,	1. John Urban	1971	Jan 19	E
	2. Richard Pius	1937	Dec 19	E
Cahouet,	Ralph Eugene	2011	Mar 13	E
Caien,	Joseph Reginald	1974	Feb 9	E
Cain,	Thomas Matthias	2000	Oct 27	S
Caldwell,	Jordan Eugene	1879	Apr 19	W
Callaghan,	Patrick John	1904	Jun 19	W
Callahan,	John Leonard	1984	Oct 22	C
Callan,	1. Charles Jerome	1962	Feb 26	E
	2. George Humbert	1971	Jan 10	E
Camilleri,	Emmanuel M.	2006	Jan 13	S
Campbell,	1. Francis Bartholomew	1930	Aug 28	E
	2. James Downey Jn Dom.	2004	Feb 11	S
	3. Robert Ignatius	2002	Jul 24	C
	4. Stuart Bede	1986	Sep 22	E
Cannon,	Leo Stephen	1978	Mar 11	E
Canton,	James Sylvester	1939	Mar 25	E

Cappellino,	Crocian Ignatius	1952	Jul 9	E
Carey,	1. Bartholomew Vincent	1873	Oct 7	E
	2. Thomas Fabian	1972	May 8	E
Carl,	Orville Theodore	1991	Apr 14	E
Carlson,	Edward Sebastian	1990	Oct 9	C
Carney,	James Timothy	1995	Aug 11	E (Pakistan)
Carolan,	Matthew Leo	1938	Jun 6	E
Carosella,	Charles Alphonsus	1985	Nov 3	S
Carpentier,	Raphael George	1967	Nov 3	C
Carr,	1. George Alphonse	1898	Mar 27	E
	2. Kevin Edmund	1986	Jul 28	W
Carrigan,	John Thaddeus	2009	Sep 7	E
Carroll,	1. Charles Bernardine	1966	Jan 30	E
	2. Phillip	1902	Dec 8	W
	3. Robert Patrick	1967	Mar 3	C
	4. Thomas Finbar	1998	Dec 8	E
	5. William Augustine	1988	Apr 24	E
	6. William Kevin	2017	Feb 19	C
Carter,	Daniel Louis	1978	Dec 19	C
Casenave,	Louis	1893	Nov 23	E
Casey,	1. Daniel Edward Mary	2000	Jan 3	E
	2. Denis Albert	1940	Mar 20	E
Cashin,	Joseph Thomas	1896	Feb 14	E
Casquero,	Froyland	1950	Jun 3	W (Spain)
Cassidy,	1. Conrad Donald	1994	Sep 14	C
	2. Felix Francis	2015	Nov 13	W
	3. Joseph Daniel	2010	Mar 28	E
	4. William Ferrer	1974	Nov 21	E
Cassin,	Martin Patrick	1892	Sep 29	W
Casterot,	Peter Alexis	1952	Jun 28	E
Cavalli,	Victor Vincent	2016	Feb 5	W
Caverly,	John Walter	1991	Sep 25	S
Celio,	Victor Francis A.	2010	Oct 19	S
Cenkner,	William Cyprian	2003	Aug 8	S
Cervera,	Raymond Cajetan	1911	Dec 7	W
Cevasco,	Raymond Ambrose	1983	Jun 3	E
Chamberlain,	Sylvester Clyde	1957	Dec 30	W
Chambers,	Dominic	1894	Feb 6	W
Champine,	Harold Vincent	2007	Dec 13	C
Champlin,	Carson Fabian	1989	Oct 7	C
Chandler,	Arthur Hyacinth	1945	Jun 29	E
Chang,	Thomas Dominic	1967	Apr 2	E
Chen,	Matthew Francis	1996	Aug 14	E
Chereso,	James Cajetan	1980	Nov 24	C

Christmas,	Charles Fidelis	1960	May 11	E
Clancy,	1. Ceslaus Thomas	1948	Dec 30	W
	2. Edward Vincent Ferrer	1973	Oct 25	E
	3. Martin Peter	1879	Jul 23	E
	4. Patrick Michael James	2001	Oct 3	C
Clark,	1. Joseph Richard	1952	Jun 30	E
	2. Louis Gerald	1945	Apr 4	W
	3. William Richard	1957	Jun 4	E
Clarke,	John Richard	1980	Dec 30	C
Clarkson,	1. James Hyacinth	1849	Aug 25	E
	2. Sydney Albert	1901	Dec 16	E
Cleary,	1. Edward Louis	2011	Nov 21	C
	2. Grattan Vincent	1927	Feb 5	E
	3. John Raymond	1855	Sep 17	E
Clifford,	1. Thomas Aquinas	2011	Jun 1	S
	2. Walter Dominic	1971	Apr 4	E
Clyne,	Bertrand Frederick	1964	Jan 11	W
Coburn,	Albert John-Marie	2001	Jun 29	S
Cochran,	George Leonard	2013	Mar 30	E
Coffey,	James Reginald	1985	Sep 6	E
Colbert,	James Francis	1931	Aug 27	E
Coll,	Peter Clement	1887	May 6	E
Collins,	1. Clement Eugene	1995	Dec 10	S
	2. George Sylvester	1883	Mar 13	E
	3. John Sylvester	1884	Jul 21	E
	4. Raymond Thomas Aq.	2000	Oct 8	E
Comeau,	James Raphael	1983	Sep 12	S
Conaty,	Patrick James	1979	Sep 18	E
Concanen,	+ Richard Luke	1810	Jun 19	E (Ireland)
Concordia,	George Lawrence	2015	Aug 20	E
Condon,	Bernard Patrick	1986	Aug 21	W
Conlan,	1. George Ignatius	1926	Jul 20	E
	2. William Pius	2000	Aug 26	S
Conley,	Wayne Edward	2010	Feb 9	S
Conlon,	Thomas Fidelis	1959	Apr 20	E
Conly,	Hugh Pius	1904	Jan 21	E
Connaughton,	George Brendan	1961	Apr 29	E
Connell,	1. Daniel John Francis	1971	Jun 29	C
	2. Michael	1902	Jun 2	E
	3. Michael Norbert	1957	Nov 30	E
	4. Vincent Edward	1972	Oct 25	E
Connelly,	1. Alexander Stephen	1968	May 21	E
	2. Stephen Thomas	1965	Dec 6	W
Connolly,	1. Bernard Mary	1948	Mar 12	W

	2. Bertrand James	1964	Oct 13	C
	3. Francis Dominic	1972	Aug 30	E
	4. James Cleophas	1973	Jul 26	E
	5. + John Dominic	1825	Feb 6	E
	6. Patrick Francis	2007	Mar 13	E
	7. Richard Brendan	1977	Apr 1	C
	8. Thomas Kevin	1975	Sep 21	E
Connors,	Joseph Martin	2010	Jun 25	E
Conroy,	John Jerome	2005	Jul 30	E
Considine,	Joseph Sylvester	1973	Feb 3	C
Conway,	1. George Gerard	1984	Jan 19	C
	2. Pierre Hyacinth	2006	Jan 23	E
	3. Robert Francis	1994	Jul 15	E
	4. Walter James	1972	Sep 22	C
Cooper,	Henry Francis	1928	Sep 18	E
Corbett,	Paul Gerald	1958	Jan 2	E
Corcoran,	1. Charles John Dominic	1984	Sep 19	C
	2. James	1878	Jan 30	E
	3. Patrick Joseph	1936	Sep 14	E
	4. Raphael Joseph	1936	May 2	W
Cordeiro,	Anthony Gilbert	2010	Sep 26	W
Corigliano,	Dominic Urban	1980	Aug 4	E
Corley,	Patrick Francis	1919	May 16	E
Corr,	John Raymond	2005	Jun 7	S
Corrigan,	John Vincent	1916	Jul 6	E
Cosgrove,	John Malachy	2011	Feb 25	S
Coskren,	Thomas Marcellus	2003	Dec 22	E
Costa,	Dominic Raymond	?	?	W
Costello,	1. John Justin	1964	Sep 12	E
	2. William Lawrence	1956	Aug 25	E
Coté,	1. Arthur Basil	1944	Jun 14	C
	2. David Aaron Joseph	2012	Jan 27	E
Coudeyre,	Joseph Cyril	1943	Mar 5	E
Coughlin,	1. Francis Nicholas	1989	Mar 1	E
	2. Daniel Peter	1940	Oct 2	E
Coverdale,	Gerald Thaddeus	2008	Jun 21	S
Cowan,	John Aquinas	1947	Oct 7	E
Coyne,	1. Matthew Francis	1855	Mar 8	E
	2. Michael Peter	1967	Oct 9	E
Craig,	Leo Peter	1951	Apr 5	E
Craven,	Edward Reginald	1976	Mar 24	E
Creahan,	Walter Lawrence	1984	Jan 23	E
Crescentio Gonzalez, Miguel		1978	Oct 13	W (Holy Rosary)
Crilly,	William Humbert	1969	Nov 17	C

Crombie,	James Gerald	1964	Feb 27	E
Cronin,	1. Paul Francis William	1981	Jul 29	E
	2. Peter Daniel	1894	Jul 19	W
Crowe,	Robert Francis	2010	Feb 16	C
Crowley,	1. Charles Bonaventure	1995	Jul 6	E
	2. Daniel Brendan	1997	Jan 6	E
	3. Dennis Dominic	1887	May 31	E
	4. Timothy Leonard	1929	Jan 18	E
Cubero,	Francis	1883	Jul 14	E
Cuddy,	Matthew Eugene	1963	Feb 9	C
Cull,	Leo Urban	1946	Sep 9	E
Cumiskey,	Thomas Malachy	2002	Aug 22	S
Cummings,	Edward Joachim	1931	Jun 18	E
Cummins,	William Gregory	1954	Aug 27	E
Cunningham,	1. Francis Louis Bertrand	1963	Sep 24	C
	2. Henry Paul	1961	Jun 6	E
	3. James Justin	1996	Oct 1	E
	4. John Fabian	2006	Dec 4	E
Curley,	John Gerard	1982	Aug 20	E
Curran,	1. Adam Paul	1953	Sep 23	E
	2. John Leonard	1972	Mar 14	C
	3. Paul Chrysostom	1995	Nov 12	E
	4. Peter Carrol	1982	Oct 27	W
	5. William John	1965	Feb 25	C
Curry,	Timothy Louis Bertrand	1990	Aug 15	S
Curtin,	Barnabas William	1987	May 21	W
Curtis,	Leonard Edward	1995	Nov 17	S
Dabash,	Adrian George	2017	Jan 27	E
Daigle,	Louis Marie	1954	Aug 22	C
Dailey,	1. George Raymond	1873	Sep 23	E
	2. Joseph Vincent	1972	Jul 24	E
	3. Thomas Humbert	1972	May 5	C
Daley,	1. Colum Dennis	1994	Feb 11	Nigeria [C]
	2. William Charles	1936	Nov 21	E
Daly,	1. + Edward Celestine	1964	Nov 23	E
	2. James Alphonse	1914	May 4	E
	3. James Vincent	1881	Jul 3	E
Damiani,	Dominic Innocent	1932	Mar 21	E
Daniel,	Louis John	1896	Jun 17	W
Danilowicz,	Richard Donald	1980	Sep 28	E
Davidson,	Albert Basil	1954	Oct 9	E
Davies,	Daniel Thaddeus	2018	Aug 2	E
Davis,	1. Clifford Leo	1984	Mar 20	E
	2. James Joseph	2011	Jul 28	E

	3. John Barnabas	2017	Nov 16	E
Dawson-Amoah,	Jude Thaddeus	2009	Jul 9	N Nigeria
De Cantillon,	Edward Pius	1900	Sep 5	E
de Wasseige,	Eric	2010	Mar 31	C (Belgium)
Delaney,	Denis Dominic	1943	Feb 4	E
Delavigne,	Charles Mannes	1969	Dec 15	E
Della Penta,	1. Daniel Mark	1978	Jan 3	C
	2. Joseph Clement	1999	Aug 28	C
Dempflin,	William	1912	Dec 3	W
Dempsey,	1. + James Michael	1996	Mar 19	C
	2. John Ambrose	1929	Nov 20	E
Denier,	Anthony Henry	2004	Apr 27	C
Dennis,	1. Charles	1995	Dec 9	W
	2. Warren Bede	1993	Nov 12	S
Derham,	Hyacinth James	1891	Dec 30	W
Dering,	Bernard John	1960	Dec 23	C
Desmond,	Joseph Richard	1996	Jan 25	E
Determan,	Joseph Humbert	2016	Oct 22	S
Devereaux,	1. James Paul	1889	Jul 31	E
	2. Simon Patrick	1864	Aug 16	E
Devine,	James Luke	1947	May 31	E
Dewdney,	Raymond Jerome	1972	Jul 22	E
Di Fede,	Thomas Vincent	2011	Apr 9	E
di Michele,	Francis Vincent	1936	Feb 21	E
Di Nardo,	Salvatore	2004	Apr 24	W
Dillon,	1. John Jordan	1944	Dec 1	E
	2. John Stanislaus	1995	Nov 30	E
	3. William Justin	1978	Jun 8	E
	4. William Raymond	1974	Jun 18	E
Dinahan,	Peter Aloysius	1904	Jan 21	E
Dinet,	John Francis	2008	Jan 2	S
Dionne,	Adelard Benedict	1982	Aug 1	E
Doane,	Willard Paul	1969	Jul 16	E
Doherty,	1. Hyacinth	1860-61	Dec ?	E
	2. Patrick Joseph	1895	Nov 6	E
	3. Peter Hyacinth	1861	Nov 3	E
	4. Sean Brendan	1996	Jul 16	W
Dolan,	1. James Linus	2018	Apr 20	S (Peru)
	2. Lawrence Richard	1964	Jun 23	E
	3. Vincent Dominic	1959	Dec 14	E
Dolehide,	John Robert	2012	Jul 27	C
Donahue,	John Matthew	1982	Sep 12	E
Donlan,	Thomas Cajetan	1999	Feb 26	C
Donlon,	Malachy	1951	Aug 14	E

Donnelly,	1. Dominic John	1960	Jan 12	W
	2. Edward Dominic	1920	Feb 16	E
	3. Thomas Chrysostom	1973	Nov 15	E
Donohue,	Dominic Innocent	1956	Mar 14	E
Donovan,	1. David Joseph	1971	Dec 3	E
	2. Edward Jordan	1956	Jan 26	E
	3. Gerald Brian	2009	Mar 21	S
	4. Vincent Clement	1977	Jan 30	E
Doogan,	Mannes Bernard	1912	Jul 2	W
Dooley,	1. John Reginald	1970	Feb 19	E
	2. Roderick Malachy	2002	Jun 15	C
	3. William Augustine	1981	Jan 13	E
	4. William Dean	1974	Feb 2	W
Dore,	Vincent Cyril	1984	Dec 14	E
Dorsey,	Edward Sylvester	1990	Oct 3	E
Dowd,	Thomas Patrick	1957	Jul 17	E
Downes,	William Louis Mary	1983	Dec 26	E
Downey,	Martin Michael	2017	Jul 15	E
Doyle,	1. Edward Paul	1997	Apr 12	E
	2. Patrick Benedict	1935	Nov 2	E
	3. Paul	1881	Oct 6	E
Drexelius,	Clement Albert	1981	Mar 7	E
Driscoll,	1. Alexius John	1967	May 1	C
	2. James Aloysius	2013	Nov 7	E
	3. Pius Francis	1941	Jan 1	W
Duffy,	1. Francis Charles	2006	Mar 21	E
	2. John Jordan	1975	Sep 19	E
Dugan,	Francis Henry	1941	Feb 20	C
Dunn,	1. Francis Joseph	1891	Feb 4	E
	2. William Reginald	1911	Jan 24	E
Duprey,	William Leo	1970	Feb 3	E
Durbin,	Walter Charles	1961	Aug 24	E
Durkin,	1. Augustine Adolph	1938	May 15	E
	2. John Ambrose	1885	Jul 31	E
	3. John Jerome	1950	Jul 1	E
Dwyer,	1. John Jordan	1943	Mar 5	E
	2. Joseph	1877	Feb 24	E
	3. Simon Thomas	1908	Feb 23	W
	4. Timothy Victor	1983	Mar 31	E
Dyson,	Thomas Augustine	1898	Oct 21	W
Eckert,	Michael Joseph	1939	Mar 26	E
Edelen,	James Vincent	1892	Nov 18	E
Egan,	1. Constantius Louis	1899	Jul 7	E
	2. James Mark	1966	Jun 15	E

	3. John Anselm	1988	Oct 9	S
	4. John Paul	1924	Mar 27	E
	5. Maurice James	?	Dec ?	E
Ehler,	Gerard William	1999	Oct 8	W
Elder,	William Peter	1984	May 3	S
Elnen,	Paul Adrian	1956	Aug 14	E
Emmans,	Philip Edward	1957	Dec 3	C
English,	Adrian Theodore	1964	Feb 29	E
Enis,	Bernard Antoninus	1938	Aug 11	E
Enright,	James Dalmatius	1970	Sep 16	E
Erwin,	James Matthew	2000	Mar 6	C
Eterovich,	Francis Hyacinth	1981	Oct 29	C (Croatia)
Eulberg,	John Thomas a'Kempis	1984	Mar 29	C
Evans,	1. Alan Augustine	1999	Nov 17	E
	2. Iltud	1972	Jul 22	W (England)
Everitt,	Edward Elms	2011	Jul 11	S
Every,	Robert Louis	2000	Apr 8	S
Fabian,	1. Andrew Cyril	2017	Jul 14	C
	2. John Charles	2014	Oct 29	C
Fahey,	James Martin	1916	Jul 8	W
Fahy,	Anthony Dominic	1871	Feb 20	E (Ireland)
Fallon,	1. John Alphonse	1944	Feb 17	E
	2. Thomas Leonard	1993	Nov 24	E
	3. Thomas Raymond	1875	Sep 9	E
Fandal,	Damian Callery	1994	Apr 22	S
Fanning,	Francis Jordan	1955	May 8	E
Farley,	Eugene Bernard	1923	Jul 20	E
Farmer,	1. Edward Joseph	1920	Jul 15	E
	2. Richard Robert	2006	Aug 18	C
Farrell,	1. Edward Paul	1989	Apr 8	E
	2. Charles Albert	2010	Mar 6	E
	3. John Peter	2003	Nov 25	E
	4. Lawrence Gerard (Kenneth)	2012	Oct 14	W
	5. Leo Louis	1953	Jul 10	E
	6. Walter Raphael	1951	Nov 23	C
	7. William Owen	1989	Feb 8	S
Faunt,	Patrick Thomas	1886	Jul 10	E
Fay,	1. Benjamin Urban	1977	Feb 7	E
	2. Edmund Gregory	2012	Jan 27	S
Fearon,	John Daniel	1992	Mar 14	W
Feehan,	Robert William	1963	Apr 19	W
Feeley,	Frederick Francis	1925	May 10	E
Feeney,	Patrick	1895	May 20	E
Feltrop,	Victor Sylvester	1984	Dec 15	C

Fennell,	Charles Vincent Ferrer	1974	Mar 15	E
Fenton,	Norman Hilarion	2011	Jun 12	E
Fenwick,	1. + Edward Dominic	1832	Sep 26	E
	2. Francis Edward Dominic	1973	Jun 24	E
	3. John Ceslaus	1815	Aug 20	E
Ferrick,	Edward Jude	1994	Jul 21	E
Ferris,	Richard George	1952	Jun 1	E
Feucht,	Thomas Bernard	1980	Jun 10	W
Figueras,	Anthony	1964	Mar 19	W (Spain)
Fihn,	Norbert D.	1994	May 30	W
Finn,	Raymond Chrysostom	2016	Jan 26	S
Fincel,	William Alphonse	1972	Aug 25	E
Finnegan,	1. Francis Xavier	1968	Aug 8	E
	2. John Theodore	1937	Oct 19	E
Finnerty,	John Lawrence	1968	Feb 22	E
Finnin,	Edward Berchmans	1991	Jul 21	E
Fisher,	John Cyril	1982	Jan 6	C
Fitzgerald,	1. Edward Gregory	1963	Feb 17	E
	2. Jeremiah Thomas	1950	May 20	E
	3. John Bertrand	1981	Apr 11	E (Ireland)
	4. John Vincent	1967	Sep 1	E
Fitzpatrick,	James Ambrose	1978	Aug 21	E
Fitzsimmons,	1. Robert Philip	2013	Feb 3	E
	2. Thomas Aquinas	1896	Nov 8	W
Flaherty,	Lawrence	1890	Jun 9	E
Flanagan,	Paul Victor	1942	Apr 3	E
Flannery,	John Charles	2013	Mar 24	W
Fleck,	Richard Ambrose	2009	Aug 7	E
Fleming,	James Andrew	1967	Jan 24	E
Flood,	Eugene Vincent	1917	Aug 2	E
Flynn,	1. Michael Benedict	1925	Dec 9	E
	2. Thomas Valerian	1997	Feb 4	C
Foerstler,	Robert Vincent	2006	Aug 4	W
Fogarty,	Joseph Charles	2016	Jan 26	C
Foley,	1. Frederick Clement	1955	Aug 17	E
	2. John Anthony	1976	Oct 2	E
	3. Martin Jordan	1945	Feb 9	E
Folsey,	William David	2018	Sep 23	E
Ford,	1. John Hyacinth	1911	Mar 4	E
	2. Richard John Thomas	1937	Dec 1	E
Forquer,	Joseph George	1990	Oct 30	C
Forster,	Cornelius Philip	1993	Nov 18	E
Fortune,	Moses Benedict	1885	Mar 13	E
Foster,	James Hyacinth	1941	Jan 23	E

Fowler,	James Dominic	1930	Feb 9	E
Fox,	1. Antoninus Francis	1954	Jul 31	C
	2. Luke Joseph	1959	Jan 8	W
Fraher,	John Sylvester	1944	Apr 19	C
France-Kelly,	Kenneth Archibold	2015	Jun 21	E
Freeman,	Hilary Justin	1998	Nov 3	C
Frenay,	Adolph Dominic	1971	Jan 19	E
Frendo.	Hyacinth Peter	1996	Sep 11	E (Rome)
Friel,	George Quentin	1974	Feb 23	E
Fritter,	Christopher Raymond	1985	May 18	W
Frusti,	David Paul	1991	Aug 1	C
Fu,	Bartholomew Paul	2001	Aug 23	E
Fulton,	Joseph John	1998	Dec 12	W
Gabisch,	Thomas Carl	1969	May 30	W
Gaffney,	1. Francis Augustine	1922	Dec 2	E
	2. James	1895	Sep 3	E
Gaines,	John Stanley	1981	Nov 28	C
Gainor,	Charles Leo	1967	Apr 18	C
Gallagher,	1. Edward Henry	2009	Nov 20	E
	2. Edward Kevin	1941	Jul 3	C
	3. Thomas Raphael	1979	Dec 10	E
Galliher,	Daniel Michael	1961	Apr 9	E
Gangloff,	Anthony Raymond	1864	Jun 9	E
Gannon,	William	2016	Jul 10	E
Garry,	Martin Edward Dominic	1973	Jun 24	E
Garvey,	John Hyacinth	1882	Feb 16	E
Gately,	Alfred Augustine	2000	Apr 7	E
Gavin,	Stephen Alphonse	1943	Oct 23	E
Gaynor,	1. Bernard Patrick	1904	Mar 3	W
	2. Thomas Patrick	1969	Jan 22	C
Geary,	1. Cyril Andrew	1977	Jul 5	C
	2. Mark Paul	1997	Sep 7	S
Georges,	1. Ferdinand Norbert	1969	Jul 7	E
	2. Irving Aloysius	1969	Mar 11	E
Geraets,	Harold Chrysostom	2001	Feb 18	C
Geraghty,	James Bernard	1860	Jul 10	E
Gerhard,	John Peter	2005	Mar 18	E
Gerlach,	Harold John Baptist	2013	Nov 21	C
Giannotti,	Damian Girard	1994	Feb 22	W
Gillespie,	Raymond Sebastian	1938	Feb 8	E
Gilligan,	Thomas Dennis	1981	Apr 17	E
Gillis,	James Raphael	1979	Mar 13	C
Gilroy,	John Clement	1935	Oct 13	E
Gilsenan,	Joseph Fidelis	1987	Sep 17	E

Ginet,	Joseph Alphonse	1934	Mar 4	E
Glennon,	William	1863	Apr 9	E
Glynn,	Andrew Dominic	1942	Dec 1	C
Gobeille,	Bertrand Alan	2002	Apr 23	C
Goedert,	Robert Alexius	2015	Dec 19	C
Goetz,	1. Stephen G.	1989	Sep 30	S
	2. William Andrew	1918	Oct 20	E
Goggin,	Richard Hyacinth	1898	Aug 5	E
Goggins,	Damian Ralph	1967	Feb 18	C
Going,	Gregory Joseph	2000	Sep 26	S
Goldrick,	Michael Quentin	1972	Aug 20	E
Gonzalez Baragano, Avelino		1992	Jun 8	S (Spain)
Gordon,	Frederick Aquinas	1974	Sep 19	E
Gore,	John Raymond	1984	Nov 29	W
Gorman,	Francis Bertrand	1948	Dec 25	E
Gorski,	1. Mark	2016	Sep 22	W
	2. Stan Edward	1978	Oct 25	C
Goss,	Joseph Urban	2006	Jun 7	S
Gough,	Patrick Simon	1863	Jul 2	E
Grace,	1. John Raymond	1980	May 21	E
	2. + Langdon Thomas	1897	Feb 22	E
Grady,	1. Edward Damian	1969	Apr 7	E
	2. Francis Leonard	1959	Apr 3	E
Graham,	1. Henry Chrysostom	1966	Jun 5	E
	2. James Gilbert	2008	Jun 20	C
Green,	Austin Edward	2014	Mar 24	S
Griego,	Carlos Vincent Ferrer	2010	Feb 18	C
Groover,	Henry B.	2017	Jan 17	S
Gruber,	Joseph Paul	1967	Jun 5	E
Guagliardo,	Vincent Anthony	1995	Aug 13	W
Gubbons,	John Dominic	1909	Jan 22	E
Guerra,	Jesús de Vianney	2014	Oct 19	S
Gunning,	James Christopher	1971	Aug 23	E
Gutierrez-Martin, Florent		1973	Sep 13	W (H. Rosary)
Hackett,	James Walter	1978	Jun 16	E
Haddad,	Norman	2016	Oct 6	E
Hagan,	Joseph Joachim	1986	Dec 29	C
Haggerty,	Leo John	1928	Jun 2	W
Hahn,	James Cornelius	2008	Nov 8	C
Haladus,	Jerome Joachim	2008	Jul 3	E
Hall,	1. Antoninus Lawrence	1981	Jun 16	W
	2. Harry Arthur	1974	Apr 1	C
	3. Ralph Theodore	2012	Jan 9	E
Halligan,	1. Nicholas Francis	1997	Jun 29	E

	2. Raymond Ferrer	2016	Mar 18	E
Hallisy,	James Benedict	1867	Dec 23	E
Halloran,	1. Gerard Eugene	1988	May 15	C
	2. Thomas Leo	1950	May 23	W
Halton,	Edward Boniface	1983	Oct 7	E
Hamel,	Anthony Henry Suso	1991	Jul 10	S
Hanley,	1. Matthew Earl	1972	Jun 2	E
	2. Philip Louis Bertrand	1982	Apr 27	E
Hanlon,	Bernard	1890	Sep 11	E
Harkins,	Bernard Kenneth	2011	Jan 27	E
Harney,	Milton John	1825	Jan 15	E
Harrington,	Edmond John	1908	Apr 15	W
Harris,	1. Joseph Francis	1957	Oct 8	C
	2. Pius Edward	1978	Aug 2	W
Hart,	Bernard George	1993	Apr 19	E
Hartigan,	Patrick Vincent	1904	Aug 5	E
Hartke,	Gilbert Vincent Ferrer	1986	Feb 21	E
Hartnett,	John Hugh	1963	Oct 24	E
Hartung,	Martin Lloyd	1990	Dec 23	C
Hasenfuss,	George Bernard	1956	Mar 17	E
Haverty,	Charles Augustine	1971	Aug 7	E
Hayes,	1. Charles Edmund	1968	Sep 11	C
	2. John Finnbarr	2017	Dec 20	W
Heagen,	Leo Matthew	1951	Sep 21	E
Healy,	1. Antoninus Albert	1959	Jun 14	W
	2. John Henry	1963	Jul 26	E
Heaney,	James Patrick	1904	Jun 22	E
Heary,	1. James Benedict	1966	Feb 11	E
	2. Walter Eusebius	1969	Mar 20	E
Heasley,	Patrick Pius	1968	May 20	E
Heath,	1. Richard Mark	2005	Dec 4	E
	2. Thomas Richard	2005	Jan 13	E
	3. Walter John	1987	Oct 24	E
Heenan,	Joseph Antoninus	1928	Mar 20	E
Heffernan,	1. Edward Matthias	1974	Jul 30	E
	2. Joseph Reginald	1923	Mar 15	E
Hegarty,	James Benedict	1943	Mar 22	C
Hennessey,	1. Robert Justin	2003	Dec 7	E
	2. Thomas Edward Dominic	1993	Jun 21	E
Henrion,	William	1872	Feb 24	E
Henry,	1. Andrew John	1971	Aug 17	C
	2. Paul Thomas	1919	Jul 31	W
	3. Ronald Hector	2012	Aug 27	S
	4. Thomas	1917	Dec 21	E

Hensley,	Leroy Gilbert	2014	May 31	C
Herlihy,	Joseph Reginald	1989	May 21	E
Herold,	George Gregory	1974	Oct 12	E
Hess,	Charles Raphael	1998	Aug 24	W
Heuschkel,	Robert Regis	2017	Jul 19	E
Hickey,	1. Frederick Cornelius	1966	Dec 25	E
	2. Thomas Anthony	1914	Dec 24	E
	3. John Daniel	1987	Jan 25	S
	4. Reginald Thomas	1888	Jun 29	W
Higgins,	1. Arthur Vincent	1917	Apr 10	E
	2. Joseph Reginald	1939	Nov 28	E
Hill,	1. John Augustine	1828	Sep 3	E
	2. William Joseph	2001	Oct 12	E
Hinch,	John Aloysius	1941	Aug 12	E
Hinnebusch,	1. Gerard Paul	2002	Aug 20	S
	2. Louis Albert	1958	Mar 10	C
	3. William Aquinas	1981	Jan 12	E
Hoban,	James Dominic	1891	Jul 23	E
Hoesli,	Frederick Damien	2015	Jun 9	E
Hoff,	Wilfred Gabriel	2014	Jul 18	C
Hoffman,	Dominic Francis	1998	Dec 6	W
Hofstee,	Leo Anthony	1986	Apr 26	W
Hogan,	Ernest Albert	1979	May 24	E
Hohman,	Henry Francis	1963	Nov 12	C
Holachek,	Terence Albert	2005	Aug 17	S
Holden,	Kieran James	1907	Apr 24	E
Holl,	Vincent George	1955	Mar 13	E
Holland,	Eugene William	1926	Nov 2	E
Holohan,	Edward Eugene	1976	Aug 11	E
Hopkins,	Martin Keith	1980	Aug 11	C
Hoppe,	Henry Joseph	1994	Aug 30	S
Horan,	Walter Hubert	1983	Apr 8	E
Horgan,	William Antoninus	1886	Nov 3	E
Horn,	Francis Gabriel	1943	Aug 3	E
Hornick,	Francis John	1888	Apr 17	W
Horrigan,	Michael Antoninus	1907	Dec 7	E
Houlihan,	Peter John	1968	Jun 14	C
Hovald,	Robert Regis	2003	May 17	C
Howley,	Francis Ambrose	1970	Feb 18	E
Hren,	Joseph Innocent	2009	Apr 12	C
Huggins,	Robert Joseph	1877	Sep 16	E
Hughes,	1. Edward Leo	1966	Mar 18	C
	2. Emmanuel Aloysius	1918	Oct 18	E
	3. Henry Benedict	1971	Jan 2	E

	4. Joseph Bernard	1944	Jul 10	E
	5. Reginald Vincent	1965	Oct 30	C
Hunt,	1. Andrew James	1929	Jan 13	W
	2. Edward Lawrence	1980	Jul 16	E
	3. Paschal Francis	1983	Jun 8	C
Hutton,	William Peter	1853	Sep 28	E
Hyde,	Joseph Eugene	1983	Nov 29	E
Hynes,	+ John Thomas	1869	Feb ?	E
Hynous,	Matthew David	2016	Mar 24	C
Ingling,	Walter Antoninus	1992	Feb 26	C
Inthout,	Hyacinth	1861	Jan 2	E
Jagoe,	1. Lawrence Edward	1951	Jun 18	W
	2. Robert Bede	2014	Aug 5	C
James,	Paul Michael	1990	Jul 1	E
Jarboe,	Joseph Thomas	1887	Mar 27	E
Jelly,	Frederick Michael	2000	Apr 14	E
Jenner,	James Stephen	2003	Jan 9	W
Joerger,	Jacob Bartholomew	2004	Jan 1	C
Johannsen,	1. Lorenz Pius	1957	Feb 28	E
	2. Randolf Bertrand	1973	May 27	E
Johns,	Raymond Henry Thomas	1902	Feb 24	W
Johnson,	Joseph Christopher	2017	Jun 17	E
Johnston,	Charles Clement	1988	Jan 15	S
Jones,	John Samuel	1905	Sep 30	W
Jordan,	1. John Aloysius	1946	Jul 23	E
	2. Martin Joseph	1962	Oct 12	E
Jorn,	Charles Sebastian	2002	Sep 25	E
Joseph,	1. Alvarus Emmanuel	1942	Dec 28	W
	2. Nadra John Benedict	2011	Nov 27	E
Joubert,	Gerard Rouleau	2004	Jan 17	S
Joyce,	1. James Gerald	1979	Jun 28	E
	2. Joseph Thomas Aquinas	1967	Nov 27	E
	3. Michael James	1864	May 3	E
Jura,	Ambrose Wilhelm	1973	Apr 15	C
Jurasko,	1. Joseph Jerome	2009	Jan 27	E
	2. Stephen Bernard	1986	Nov 11	E
Jurgelaitis,	Anthony Antoninus	2000	Oct 14	E
Justa,	Thomas Hyacinth	1911	Apr 7	E
Kalinowski,	Anthony Donald	1997	Mar 22	C
Kane,	1. Cyril Raymond	1930	Mar 17	W
	2. Dennis Cornelius	1997	Jan 5	E
	3. Dennis Patrick	1964	Oct 18	W
	4. John Victor	1991	Jan 1	W
	5. Thomas Cornelius	2009	Mar 1	E

	6. William Humbert	1970	Jun 10	C
Kaszczuk,	John Hyacinth	1940	Jul 12	E
Kaufman,	Thomas Hilary	1995	Dec 22	E
Kavanah,	Raymond Eugene	1955	Apr 24	C
Kavanaugh,	1. John Dominic James	1948	Sep 24	C
	2. Michael Andrew	1974	Jul 14	C
Keane,	John Dominic	1940	Mar 17	E
Kearney,	1. James Clement	1960	Dec 5	E
	2. James Dominic	1894	May 21	E
	3. John Dominic	1989	Apr 13	E
	4. Lawrence Francis	1924	Nov 25	E
	5. Thomas Lawrence	2010	Nov 27	C
Keating,	James Dominic	2005	Jul 11	E
Keefer,	John Edward	2008	Dec 17	S
Keelty,	Joseph Thomas	1916	Aug 27	E
Keenan,	1. Francis Gerald	1929	Feb 21	E
	2. Thomas Lawrence	1845-48	Dec ?	E
Keheeley,	John Antoninus	1902	May 12	E
Keitz,	Bernard Lawrence	2011	Oct 6	E
Kelleher,	Raphael John	1961	Jul 19	C
Kelly,	1. Ernest Francis	2002	Oct 14	E
	2. Francis Louis	1932	Feb 9	E
	3. Francis Louis	1977	Feb 26	E
	4. Henry Arthur	1976	Oct 15	E
	5. Humbert Henry	1954	Sep 28	W
	6. James Bernard	1964	Mar 5	E
	7. James Brendan	1998	Jan 13	C
	8. John Bertrand	1925	Mar 16	E
	9. John Dominic	1937	Jul 16	E
	10. Joseph Augustine	1885	Aug 7	E
	11. Joseph Leo	1981	May 27	S
	12. Luke Andrew	1972	Aug 26	W
	13. Paschal Francis	1975	Feb 7	C
	14. Patrick John	1983	Dec 16	W
	15. Thomas Benedict	1971	Jan 6	E
	16. + Thomas Cajetan	2011	Dec 14	E
	17. William Charles	1944	Apr 26	E
Kennedy,	1. Daniel Jerome	2002	Sep 25	E
	2. Daniel Joseph	1930	Apr 11	E
	3. James Reginald	1929	Dec 29	E
	4. John Justin	1951	Nov 22	E
	5. John Stanislaus	1962	Apr 8	E
	6. Louis Damian	1919	Mar 4	E
	7. Michael Joachim	1925	Jun 6	E

Kenny,	1. Basil Edward	1925	Feb 11	W
	2. Bernard David	1995	Dec 15	E
	3. John Paulinus	1992	Jan 31	E
	4. Joseph Hilary	1995	Aug 15	E
	5. Joseph Peter	2013	Jan 28	C
Kent,	John Clement	1907	Nov 26	E
Keogh,	Patrick Vincent	1896	Oct 7	E
Kernan,	1. Arthur Clement	1911	Feb 26	E
	2. Joseph Edward	1928	Jul 4	E
Kiefer,	Joseph Clertus	2012	Aug 31	W
Kienberger,	Vincent Ferrer Leo	1963	Apr 9	C
Kiesling,	Christopher Gerald	1986	Sep 2	C
Kilbridge,	Robert Antoninus	2011	Mar 5	C
Kilkenny,	James Louis Bertrand	1985	Feb 15	E
Killian,	Herman Martin	1968	Sep 15	E
King,	1. Bernard Gerald	1984	Feb 4	E
	2. John Dominic	1962	Mar 20	E
	3. Richard Raymond	1979	Jan 2	E
Kinsella,	1. George Thomas	1959	May 18	C
	2. Leo Arthur	2008	Apr 6	C
Kircher,	Joseph Bernard	1939	Jul 12	E
Klaia,	John Joseph	2003	Nov 14	W
Klapperich,	Giles Alfred	2015	Dec 19	C
Klueg,	Frederick Eugene	1988	Apr 18	C
Knauff,	Gabriel Mary Aloysius	1962	Apr 4	W
Kneip,	Dominic M.	1877	Oct 4	E
Kocchi,	Glenn	1967	Dec 23	C
Konkel,	Joseph Denis	2013	Nov 3	S
Kopfman,	1. George Hyacinth	1972	Jul 28	E
	2. William Ferrer	1988	Jan 3	E
Kowalkowski,	Bruno Hyacinth	1998	Aug 10	C
Kraft,	Thomas Dominic	2009	Jan 22	W
Krish,	Laurence Frank	1981	Feb 27	C
Kroeger,	Gerald Louis Bertrand	2004	Feb 23	C
Kroutch,	Anthony Ambrose	1980	Jul 22	W
Krukonis,	Richard Edward	1995	Jul 22	E
Kusmierz,	John	1984	Feb 11	E
Kyte,	Michael Gerard	2014	Mar 27	C
LaBelle,	Patrick Leo	2017	Dec 11	W
LaFrance,	Fred Valerian	2011	Jul 2	E
La More,	Edward Constantius	1958	Aug 11	E
La Plante,	Ralph Augustine	1921	Nov 4	E
Lacey,	John Jordan	1988	Nov 18	E
Lamarre,	Ambrose	1940	May 19	W (Canada)

Lamb,	Christopher Vincent	1962	Mar 6	W
Lamberty,	James Peter Philip	2008	Jul 17	S
LaMotte,	Victor Samuel	1999	May 19	C
Lanctot,	William Vincent	1936	Jan 26	E
Landy,	Edgar Regis	1947	Dec 27	E
Lane,	Gabriel Robert	1974	Jun 10	C
Lannen,	Joseph William	1935	Mar 29	E
Larcher,	Fabian Richard	1991	Feb 14	S
Larnen,	John Brendan	1992	Jul 20	E
Larpenteur,	Roscoe Francis	1947	Apr 27	C
Lavigne,	Robert Henry	2001	Apr 15	W
Lawler,	1. Albert Sadoc Patrick	1932	Mar 7	W
	2. William Raymond	1964	Aug 15	C
Lawton,	+ Thaddeus Edward	1966	Dec 19	C
Leahy,	1. Michael	1909	Aug 12	E
	2. Thomas Paul	2003	Feb 17	C
Leary,	Edmund Barnabas	1977	Aug 12	E
Lehner,	Francis Christopher	1979	Feb 24	E
Leibold,	Francis	2007	Apr 5	E
Lennon,	Joseph Luke	2011	Jun 21	E
Lentz,	Dominic Joseph	1883	Jul 8	W
Leonard,	Hugh John	1930	Oct 4	E
Leuer,	Mark R.	1992	Dec 3	S
Level,	Ferdinand Gaston	1952	Mar 8	E
Lewis,	1. Antoninus Regis	1938	Aug 25	W
	2. Raymond Leo	1969	Jul 12	W
	3. William Thomas	1978	Apr 30	W
Lillie,	Camillus Edward	1966	May 20	C
Lilly,	1. Hugh Francis	1914	Dec 3	E
	2. Michael Dominic	1901	Aug 20	E
Linahan,	William Francis	1917	Nov 25	E
Lindsay,	Robert Lawrence	1969	Feb 3	W
Lindsey,	Ambrose	1890	Aug 5	E
Lister,	Alfred Quentin	1997	Aug 16	S
Litzinger,	Charles Ignatius	1966	Nov 18	E
Locchetto,	John Jude	2014	Oct 29	E
Lockingen,	Leonard Joseph	1911	Jun 16	E
Logan,	1. Francis Bernard	1922	Mar 9	E
	2. John Berchmans	1953	May 21	E
	3. William John Dominic	2012	Jun 6	S
Lombard,	Michael	1869	Apr 15	E
Lonergan,	John James	1980	Jul 28	E
Long,	Richard	1973	Mar 19	E
Lord,	Matthew Raymond	1969	Jun 14	W

Lucier,	Charles Valerian	1997	Nov 20	E
Lux,	Lawrence Vincent Ferrer	1989	Feb 17	S
Lynch,	1. John Hyacinth	1908	Aug 7	E
	2. Patrick Louis	1886	Mar 30	E
Lyons,	1. John Luke	1978	Jan 6	C
	2. Robert Gregory	1955	Feb 9	E
Mackin,	James Andrew	1938	Nov 13	E
MacLeay,	Richard Paul	2010	Jan 13	S
Madden,	1. Daniel Dalmatius	2004	Dec 30	S
	2. Francis	1892	May 14	E
	3. Joseph Eugene	1977	Nov 12	E
Madigan,	John Alphonsus	2011	Feb 16	E
Madrick,	John Justin	1980	Jul 6	S
Magee,	John James	1868	Sep 17	E
Maguire,	1. Francis Hyacinth	2006	Apr 19	E
	2. Robert Reginald	1961	Jul 2	E
Maher,	1. Dominic John	1950	Dec 16	W
	2. Patrick Anthony	1952	Jan 6	E
Mahler,	Lloyd Albert	1995	Aug 5	E
Mahoney,	1. John	1883	Mar 4	E
	2. John Joseph	1990	Oct 24	E
	3. John Paul	1996	Jul 7	E
	4. William Bertrand	1980	Dec 16	C
	5. William Reginald	1935	Apr 15	E
Malatesta,	Charles Reginald	2001	Sep 17	C
Maley,	George Gerard	2009	Dec 27	E
Malone,	John Dominic	1993	Mar 7	C
Maloney,	James Raymond	1974	Dec 15	E
Malvey,	Joseph Bernard	1977	Sep 23	C
Mancinelli,	Leon	2001	Aug 22	E
Manning,	1. Joseph Adrian	1972	Jul 7	E
	2. Peter Valerian	1989	Jun 5	E
Marchant,	William Antoninus	1938	Jun 30	E
Marion,	Francis James	1888	Apr 10	W
Marr,	John Edmund	1992	May 29	C
Marrin,	William Dalmatius	1982	Jun 27	E
Martin,	1. Bertrand Valentine	1933	Sep 29	W
	2. Edward Augustine	1946	Aug 7	E
	3. Edward Louis	2000	Aug 23	E
	4. Gerard Walter	1981	Nov 12	W
	5. Hyacinth Lawrence	1940	May 10	E
	6. Thomas	1859	May 10	E
	7. Thomas William	1995	Dec 16	S
	8. Vincent James	1967	Jul 7	E

Martineau,	Charles Damian	1980	Jan 23	E
Masterson,	1. Edwin Ignatius	1984	Dec 15	E
	2. John Gerald	1993	Aug 27	S
	3. Robert Reginald	1996	Mar 28	S
Matanic,	George Michael	2013	Jul 16	W
Mattingly,	Julius Martin	1991	May 25	E
Mazzuchelli,	Samuel Charles	1864	Feb 23	E
McAllister,	Peter Thomas	1944	Aug 29	E
McAndrew,	Thomas Clement	1986	Jan 6	C
McAvey,	James Richard	2001	May 7	E
McBride,	Hugh Gregory	1964	Oct 25	E
McBrien,	Thomas Hugh	1988	Sep 9	E
McCabe,	1. Anthony Gerald	1965	Sep 22	E
	2. Bernard Christopher	2004	Oct 5	E
	3. James Anselm	1982	Jul 8	E
	4. Raymond Martin	2005	Nov 22	E
	5. Stephen Terence Chrysler	2008	Feb 26	W
McCadden,	John Francis	1959	Sep 11	E
McCaffrey,	1. Arthur Ralph	1964	Sep 16	E
	2. Michael Luke	1981	Jul 27	E
McCann,	1. Paul Donald	1976	Mar 26	W
	2. Roland Jerome	1976	Sep 2	E
McCarthy,	1. Lorenzo Cornelius	1941	Jun 28	E
	2. Thomas Bertrand	1986	Mar 23	E
McClory,	William	1972	Jan 28	W
McCormack,	Joseph Stephen	1967	Mar 4	E
McCormick,	Francis Martin	2008	Jul 24	C
McDermott,	1. Edward Aquinas	1981	Aug 28	E
	2. John Paul	1957	Jul 1	E
	3. Martin Ambrose	1971	Aug 4	C
	4. Richard Mannes	1957	Nov 28	E
	5. Stanislaus William	1945	Oct 17	W
	6. Terence Stephen	1963	Apr 5	E
McDonald,	1. Chrysostom Joseph	1953	Nov 15	C
	2. Edward Martin	1995	Oct 30	E
	3. John James	1996	Dec 20	C
McDonnell,	1. Cyprian Edward	1935	Sep 26	W
	2. John Francis Henry	1988	May 11	C
McDonough,	James Celestine	1967	Mar 29	E
McEachen,	Colin Vincent	1993	Jul 18	W
McEachern,	Stephen Alexander	1989	Aug 19	W
McElhatton,	Thomas Horace	1965	Oct 10	W
McEneaney,	Arthur Lambert	1978	Feb 28	E
McEniry,	Edmund Ceslaus	1977	Dec 4	E

McEvoy,	Arthur Pius	1964	Sep 30	E
McFadden,	Joseph Albert	1948	Jan 19	E
McFeely,	Michael Antoninus	1908	Aug 27	E
McGarry,	Thomas Columba	1988	Mar 2	C
McGarvey,	John Raymond	1878	Aug 29	E
McGee,	James Adrian	1993	Feb 8	E
McGinley,	Hugh Hilary	1990	May 2	E
McGinnis,	Edward Sylvester	1935	Apr 28	E
McGlynn,	Thomas Matthew	1977	Sep 3	E
McGonagle,	1. Charles Clement	1960	May 13	E
	2. Raymond Stephen	1963	Aug 13	E
McGonigle,	Thomas Declan	2015	Aug 4	C
McGovern,	1. Anthony John	1932	Oct 22	E
	2. James Benedict	1918	Sep 21	E
	3. John Patrick	2005	Aug 16	E
	4. Michael Joseph	2017	Nov 15	C
	5. Thomas Sylvester	1921	Apr 5	E
McGowan,	1. Edward Marcellus	1980	Mar 12	S
	2. Thomas Ceslaus	1996	Sep 13	E
McGrady,	John Hyacinth	1838	Dec 28	E
McGrane,	Dominic James	1862	May 31	E
McGrath,	1. Jordan Anthony	2018	Aug 5	C
	2. Matthew Francis	1870	Dec 15	E
McGreal,	Michael Dominick	1998	Nov 21	C
McGreevy,	1. John Gerald	2016	Jul 21	C
	2. Thomas More James	2012	Feb 3	W
McGregor,	1. George Celestine	1976	Feb 8	E
	2. John Thomas	1968	Mar 21	E
McGroarty,	Joseph Bede	2007	Apr 3	E
McGuiness,	Joseph Ignatius	1994	Nov 23	E
McGuire,	John Patrick	2016	Dec 25	E
McGwin,	James Bartholomew	1940	Dec 10	E
McHatton,	James Stanislaus	1997	Jun 16	S
McHenry,	Vincent Ferrer	2014	Feb 15	E
McHugh,	John Ambrose	1950	Apr 9	E
McInerney,	James Arthur	1980	Nov 9	C
McInnes,	Valentine Ambrose	2011	Nov 22	S
McInnis,	John Joseph	1968	Oct 10	E
McIntyre,	William Peter	1942	Sep 3	C
McKenna,	1. Charles Hugh	1980	Feb 7	E
	2. Charles Hyacinth	1917	Feb 21	E
	3. Francis Clement	1973	Feb 6	E
	4. James Thomas à Kempis	1965	Sep 15	E
	5. Patrick	1852	Oct 16	E

	6. Paul Charles	1990	Jul 4	E
McKenney,	James Luke	1974	Jul 30	E
McKeon,	Arthur Angelus John	1965	May 3	W
McLarney,	James John	1969	Nov 5	E
McLaughlin,	1. Bernard Aloysius	1953	Jun 4	E
	2. John Benedict	1869	Oct 26	E
	3. William Joseph	1958	Dec 3	E
McLoughlin,	William Athanasius	1977	Feb 28	E
McMahon,	1. Arthur Lawrence	1952	May 8	E
	2. John Anthony	2011	Sep 9	E
	3. John Donald	1962	Oct 2	E
McManus,	1. Hugh Joseph	1937	Jun 16	E
	2. Hugh Justin	1979	Oct 15	E
	3. James Ferrer	1975	Nov 29	E
McMullan,	Gerard Edward	1950	Nov 23	W
McMullen,	Brendan Jerome	2005	Feb 21	C
McNamara,	Dennis Ambrose	1969	Jul 25	C
McNerney,	John Patrick	1952	Jul 28	E
McNicholas,	1. + John Timothy	1950	Apr 22	E
	2. Michael Thomas	1947	May 1	E
	3. Michael Thomas	1968	Jun 1	C
	4. William Raymond	1987	Nov 8	S
McPhee,	Mark Douglas	1994	Jul 7	W
McQuillan,	Andrew Richard	1971	Dec 23	E
McShane,	1. Francis Dominic	1938	Feb 9	E
	2. John Albert	1882	Jun 30	E
McTigue,	Joseph Aloysius	1981	Jul 2	E
McVey,	Thomas Chrysostom	2009	Jun 29	E
Meagher,	1. Dennis Joseph	1896	Aug 10	E
	2. James Raymond	1889	Nov 1	E
	3. James Raymond	1954	Oct 19	E
	4. Paul Kevin	1976	Dec 31	W
Meagles,	Hyacinth Alfred	1922	Jan 5	W
Meaney,	Richard Jerome	1946	Apr 3	E
Meehan,	William Cyprian	1971	Nov 17	E
Mercier,	Alexander	1929	Jan 9	E
Metzger,	Charles Vincent	1890	Feb 18	E
Miles,	1. Peter Patrick	1984	Aug 15	W
	2. + Richard Pius	1860	Feb 21	E
Miller,	Robert Joachim	2005	Jul 27	C
Milmore,	Frederick Alan	1982	Apr 19	E
Minichiello,	Michael Jordan	1969	Jan 29	E
Mitchell,	1. James Louis	1957	Feb 28	E
	2. Joseph James	1939	Feb 22	W

	3. Reginald John	1970	Jan 18	W
Molloy,	John Joseph	1961	Oct 31	E
Monaghan,	Raphael	1966	Jul 21	C
Monckton,	Eugene Charles	1959	Dec 12	C
Monroe,	John Francis	1971	Nov 15	E
Montgomery,	1. Charles Pius	1860	Apr 9	E
	2. Richard Benedict	1840	Mar 9	E
	3. Samuel Louis	1863	Nov 26	E
	4. Stephen Hyacinth	1855	Feb ?	E
Moore,	1. Charles Gabriel	1949	May 11	E
	2. Gregory James	2016	Apr 16	C
	3. Thomas Clark Alexander	2009	Jul 5	C
Moraczewski,	Albert Stephen	2008	May 1	S
Morahan,	Gerald Bertrand	1998	Jun 4	C
Moran,	1. D.	1845-48	Dec ?	E
	2. John Pius	1912	Dec 17	E
	3. John Stephen	1953	Jan 8	E
	4. Walter Gregory	1956	Sep 12	E
Moreno,	Antonio	1995	Feb 18	W
Morgenthaler,	John Norbert	2004	Jul 30	S
Moriarty,	1. Edward Quentin	2003	Mar 22	C
	2. William David	1990	Jul 29	E
Morrin,	John	1843	Sep 29	E
Morris,	1. Albion Benedict	1987	Jan 7	W
	2. George Dominic	1982	Aug 14	E
	3. Michael	2016	Jul 15	W
	4. Robert Alan	2015	Mar 2	E
Morrison,	1. Colman Bonaventure	1973	Jul 20	E
	2. Robert Alan	2015	Mar 2	E
	3. Thomas Aquinas	2014	Apr 1	C
	4. Thomas Arnold	1989	Dec 27	E
Morrissey,	John Peter	1960	Nov 21	E
Morry,	Matthew Flavian	2008	May 25	E
Moschini,	Christopher Hugo	2001	Jul 31	W
Motl,	James Raymond	`2016	Apr 22	C
Mottey,	William George	1960	Dec 1	E
Moyna,	James Moneta	2005	Dec 2	E
Mueller,	Dionysius Joseph	1962	Jun 9	W
Mulcahy,	James Hilary	1974	Apr 1	E
Mulgrew,	John Bernard	1991	May 26	E
Mulhern,	1. Joseph Hugh	2008	Sep 14	E
	2. Philip Fabian	1984	Jul 25	E
Mulholland,	J.	1845-48	Dec ?	E
Mulkeen,	John Patrick	2000	Mar 20	C

Mullahy,	Patrick Dominic	1937	Oct 28	E
Mullaney,	1. Thomas Gregory	1973	Aug 21	E
	2. Thomas Urban	1989	Dec 18	E
Muller,	1. Albert Thomas	1966	Dec 20	W
	2. James	2017	Aug 24	E
Mullin,	Francis Raymond	2009	Apr 14	E
Mulvey,	1. Charles Matthew	1961	Feb 19	E
	2. Wilfred Robert	1967	Oct 4	C
Mulvin,	John Thomas	1947	Apr 29	E
Muñoz,	Raphael	1830	Jul 18	E
Murphy,	1. James Martin	1956	Aug 7	E
	2. James Michael	1992	Jan 12	E
	3. John	1959	Jan 10	E
	4. John James	1975	May 17	E
	5. John Thaddeus	2017	Jan 17	E
	6. Joseph Thomas	1893	May 29	E
	7. Patrick Francis	1909	May 2	E
	8. Pius John	1921	Mar 28	W
	9. Richard Thomas Aquinas	1998	Dec 31	S
	10. Timothy Joachim	1965	Apr 12	E
	11. William Bonaventure	1982	May 2	C
Murray,	1. Bernard Charles	1946	Apr 3	C
	2. James Stephen	2014	Dec 17	E
	3. John Thomas	1975	Aug 27	E
	4. Michael Anselm	1957	Dec 28	E
	5. Stephen Eugene	1952	Dec 1	C
Murtaugh	1. John Anthony	1947	Dec 23	C
	2. Walter Angelus	1983	May 31	E
Musselman,	Camillus Albert	1983	Nov 21	E
Myers,	1. Bernardine Benjamin	1949	Jan 11	C
	2. Chester Adrian	1968	Dec 28	C
Myett,	Robert Damian	2018	Jul 16	E
Myhan,	John Augustine	1992	May 23	W
Nagle,	1. Edward Urban	1965	Mar 11	E
	2. Thomas Clement	1993	Jul 9	E
Naselli,	Augustine Louis	1969	Mar 9	W
Nash,	Peter Francis	1968	May 20	E
Neal,	Albert Hilary	1986	Jan 3	E
Nealis,	John Thomas	1864	Mar 19	E
Nealy,	Francis Dominic	1999	Nov 12	E
Nelan,	Maurice Daniel	1992	Apr 3	E
Netterville,	Augustine William	1954	Sep 2	W
Neu,	William Reginald	2016	Oct 20	C
Newell,	Reginald James	1932	Apr 28	W

Newman,	1. Francis Daniel	1963	Feb 19	E
	2. William Andrew	2009	Apr 28	E
Nieser,	Albert Bertrand	1987	Feb 25	C
Nintemann,	Bernard George	1996	Nov 30	C
Nogar,	Jude Raymond	1967	Nov 17	C
Noon,	1. Dominic Hyacinth	1894	Sep 18	E
	2. Dominic William	1952	Jul 4	C
	3. Philip Dominic	1859	Feb 14	E
Norton,	1. Alfred Anthony	1989	Feb 25	S
	2. John Charles	2009	Jul 23	S
	3. William Aquinas	1978	Oct 2	W
Nouza,	Frank Marcolinus	2015	Feb 19	C
Novacki,	Michael Leo	2000	Mar 25	E
Nowlen,	1. John Andrew	1969	Mar 21	E
	2. Joseph Clement	1941	Jun 8	E
Nugent,	1. Emmanuel Louis	1968	Jun 5	C
	2. Marcellus John	1972	Jul 3	C
Nuttall,	1. James Vincent	2009	Mar 28	E (Pakistan)
	2. Raymond Peter	1968	May 20	E
Nwaibc,	Julius Chibuzor	2014	Sep 10	N (Nigeria)
Nyawir,	Paul Okello	2002	Aug 28	E (Kenya)
O'Beirne,	1. Aloysius	1975	Jul 21	E
	2. William Mannes	1996	Oct 16	E
O'Brien,	1. Arthur Theophane	1980	Feb 28	E
	2. Charles Henry	2014	Nov 18	E
	3. Damian Joseph	1931	Jun 3	W
	4. Dennis Augustine	1873	Oct 9	E
	5. Francis Michael	1871	Mar 15	E
	6. James Albert	1933	Jul 9	E
	7. John Pius	1993	Oct 1	S
	8. Louis Michael	1939	Jun 14	E
	9. Matthew Anthony	1871	Jan 15	E
	10. Peter Ralph	1971	Jan 6	C
O'Callahan,	John Henry	1967	Dec 11	E
O'Carroll,	+ William Dominic	1880	Oct 13	E (Ireland)
O'Connell,	1. Charles John	1955	Oct 20	E
	2. David Arthur	1994	Feb 6	E
	3. Francis Kevin	2008	Nov 4	E
	4. Francis Louis Bertrand	1969	Sep 24	E
	5. John Edmund	1994	Dec 27	S
	6. John Gerard	2001	Nov 3	C
	7. John Hyacinth	1892	Apr 29	E
	8. Joseph Sebastian	1956	Aug 4	E
	9. Robert Regis	1984	Mar 20	E

	10. William Anthony	1945	Dec 1	E
O'Connor,	1. Benedict John	1935	Jan 31	W
	2. Bertrand	1992	Jan 28	E
	3. David Gregory	1949	Jun 6	E
	4. John Bonaventure	1926	Apr 26	E
	5. John Raphael	1960	Mar 1	E
	6. Matthias Patrick	1998	Jan 7	S
	7. Michael Augustine	1957	Sep 14	E
	8. Thomas Matthew	1971	Feb 7	E
	9. Timothy Albert	1960	Jul 27	E
	10. William Francis	1932	Oct 19	E
O'Daniel,	Victor Francis	1960	Jun 12	E
O'Donnell,	1. James Andrew	1947	Oct 2	C
	2. James Gerard	1949	Aug 20	E
	3. William Jordan	1995	May 7	E
O'Dowd,	Gerald Mark	1964	Oct 23	E
O'Dwyer,	James Aloysius	1896	Aug 4	E
O'Hara,	Michael	1974	Jun 2	W
O'Hearn,	John Edward	1970	May 27	E
O'Keefe,	Anthony Patrick	1917	Apr 10	W
O'Leary,	1. Daniel Joseph	1835	Feb 8	E
	2. Jerome Aquinas	2002	Aug 28	C
	3. Louis Maurice	1974	Sep 12	E
	4. William Joseph	1941	May 18	E
O'Mahoney,	Jeremiah Clement	1911	Nov 18	E
O'Neil,	1. Arthur Charles	1920	Apr 24	E
	2. Francis Andrew	1909	May 6	E
	3. Francis Xavier	1940	Jul 6	E
O'Neill,	1. James Louis	1904	Jan 28	E
	2. Thomas Edward	1903	Dec 10	W
O'Riley,	Robert Francis Bernard	2008	Mar 14	C
O'Rourke,	1. David Kevin	2012	Mar 28	C
	2. Richard Peter	1899	Mar 5	E
	3. Timothy Peter	1913	Feb 13	W
	4. William Martin	1912	Jul 9	E
O'Shaughnessy,	William Terence	1998	Jun 27	E
O'Sullivan,	Michael Paul	1920	Jun 8	E
O'Toole,	Edward Joseph	1958	May 9	E
Odey,	Paul Ogbogu	1996	Jul 29	N (Nigeria)
Okwesili,	Godwin	2005	Aug 2	N (Nigeria)
Olsen,	Stanislaus Edward	1962	Nov 9	W
Olson,	William Jerome	1956	Apr 13	E
Osbourn,	1. Matthew Leo	1961	Dec 9	E
	2. Sydney James Cyril	1969	Dec 13	E

Osbourne,	1. Louis Bertrand	2016	Jun 16	E
	2. Thomas Antoninus	1859	May 2	E
Ostdiek,	Harold Dana	2009	May 26	C
Osunwoke,	Chukwunonye Linus	2018	Feb 17	N (Nigeria)
Outwater,	William John	1979	Jan 29	E
Owens,	1. James William	1969	Jun 17	E
	2. Sebastian John	1946	Apr 14	W
Palmer,	Humbert Vincent	1956	Feb 21	W
Pandolfo,	Lawrence L.	2009	Aug 2	S
Parent,	Octave Damian	1969	Jun 7	E
Parmisano,	Fabian Stan	2009	Jun 18	W
Parsons,	Samuel Raymond	2011	Oct 4	W
Pastorelli,	Joseph Louis	1952	May 20	E
Patrick,	Richard Martin Cletus	2015	Nov 24	S
Patten,	William Leo	1992	Apr 6	E
Paulis,	George Bonaventure	1956	Jul 13	E
Payne,	Arthur Joseph	2011	Jul 24	E
Pelick,	Loren M.	2009	Oct 9	S
Peña,	Vicente M.	2009	Jan 15	S
Pender,	James Joachim	1969	May 20	C
Pendergast,	1. Joseph Damian	1942	May 3	E
	2. Slyvester Ambrose	1888	Jul 3	E
Pendis,	Philip Bennett	1961	Oct 20	C
Perdigon,	Felix Gregory	1990	Jan 14	W
Perrotta,	Paul Christopher	1969	Nov 1	E
Perry,	1. Anthony George	1876	Nov 8	W
	2. Dominic Frederick	1939	Aug 25	E
Peterson,	1. John Stephen	2017	Jan 11	E
	2. Thomas Reginald	2000	Oct 22	E
Philibert,	Paul Joseph	2016	Apr 14	S
Phillips,	1. Edward Leonard	1967	Aug 24	E
	2. John	1923	Jul 20	E
Pidcock,	Gerald Jude	2003	Nov 9	C
Piec,	Wenceslaus John	1958	Mar 10	C
Pieper,	Robert Ferrer	1998	Aug 19	C
Pikell,	Edward Donald	1998	Jan 31	C
Pino,	Joseph Christopher	1958	Jul 21	E
Pitt,	Peter	1861	Nov 2	E
Poelking,	Joseph	1866	Dec ?	E
Polin,	Thomas James	1838	Dec 25	E
Pope,	Andrew Francis	1943	Oct 31	W
Powell,	Austin Ralph	2001	Jun 12	C
Power,	Thomas Louis	1906	Oct 20	E
Powers,	1. John Aquinas	2010	Oct 19	S

	2. Maurice Peter	1890	May 22	E
Prazan,	Robert Ceslaus	1998	Jul 5	C
Precourt,	Joseph Gerard	1968	Sep 25	E
Pritzl,	Kurt John	2011	Feb 21	E
Prout,	Francis Robert	1988	Feb 14	E
Provenzale,	Charles	1972	Nov 12	E
Purchase,	William Thomas	1953	Mar 30	E
Purtill,	Philip Daniel	1955	Dec 31	W
Putz,	Edward Hyacinth	1984	Oct 5	E
Quinlan,	Edward Timothy	1964	Jul 17	E
Quinn,	1. Antoninus James	1961	Jan 29	C
	2. Francis Theodore	1916	Sep 1	E
	3. Frank Currier Malachy	2008	Oct 31	C
	4. Robert Gabriel	1987	Jan 3	E
	5. William	1919	May 30	E
Quirk,	Charles Bernardine	1972	Dec 13	E
Rabadan,	Reginald John	1967	Aug 18	C (Croatia)
Rabbitte,	Timothy Martin	1922	Mar 20	E
Raetz,	Vincent Marcellus	1983	Jul 31	E
Raferty,	Thomas Paul Chrysostom	2018	Apr 11	W
Ralph,	Hubert Pius	1908	Feb 26	E
Ramos Y Gomez	Perez, Ferdinand	1962	Nov 12	W (Mexico)
Rascher,	Ralph Marcolinus	1980	May 7	E
Reardon,	1. John Ignatius	2004	Nov 22	S
	2. Joseph Innocent	1977	Nov 1	C
Reddy,	John Anthony	1919	Nov 27	E
Redmond,	1. Francis Stephen	1984	Jun 6	S
	2. Patrick	1873	Apr 27	E
Reese,	John Brendan	1970	Oct 3	E
Regan,	1. Ambrose Paschal	1957	Dec 21	E
	2. Francis Leo	1995	Dec 22	E
	3. James Joseph	1976	Jan 3	C
	4. James Wilfrid Matthew	2000	Mar 30	C
Reichert,	1. Charles Valerian	1997	Jan 17	E
	2. John Jordan	1987	Jun 13	E
Reid,	1. John Patrick	1985	May 14	E
	2. Nicholas Robert	1996	Aug 18	E
Reidy,	John Joseph Stephen	1977	Dec 15	C
Reilly,	1. Daniel Flavian	1962	Oct 5	E
	2. George Cajetan	1972	Nov 20	E
	3. Joseph Michael	1975	Dec 5	E
	4. Matthew Vincent	1999	Sep 1	E
	5. Peter Philip	1992	Jan 27	E
	6. Robert Donald	1992	Dec 19	E

	7. Terrence John	2016	Aug 30	W
	8. Thomas a'Kempis	1957	May 30	C
Reinhart,	Albert	1913	May 27	E
Reisdorf,	John Vincent	1891	Dec 22	E
Rennar,	Anthony William	1992	Sep 1	E
Reville,	Emile Dalmatius	1879	Sep 26	E (France)
Reynolds,	1. Francis Norbert	1972	Jul 13	E
	2. George John Dominic	2016	Jan 13	C
Ricarby,	William Ignatius	1901	Jul 5	E
Rice,	Stephen John	1934	Sep 17	W
Richmeier,	Arthur Cornelius	1986	Dec 7	C
Riley,	1. Alphonsus Peter	1932	Oct 24	W
	2. Robert Dennis	2006	Dec 28	E
Ripple,	Michael Joseph	1938	Nov 29	E
Roach,	1. George William	1955	Apr 13	C
	2. John Paul	1940	Aug 2	E
Robbilard,	George Maurice	1997	Jan 18	E
Robert,	Clarence Gabriel	1935	Jan 11	E
Roberts,	John Isidore	1971	Aug 23	C
Robinson,	1. Edward Mathias	2012	Mar 29	S
	2. Louis James	1970	Apr 8	W
Rochford,	John Antoninus	1896	Oct 5	E
Rocks,	1. Daniel Alexander	1922	Oct 1	E
	2. Owen Edmund	1966	Jul 8	E
Rogawski,	Ralph Bartholomew	2012	Feb 6	S
Rogers,	Paul Edmund	1975	Mar 27	E
Romero,	Joseph Filadelfio	2003	Dec 27	W
Roney,	Willard Patrick	1988	Mar 5	C
Rooden,	Mark James	1945	Aug 2	W
Rooney,	1. Charles Celestine	1981	Feb 23	E
	2. James Antoninus	1905	Feb 22	E
Ross,	Leo Dominic	1988	Mar 17	E
Rossetti,	Salvatore Joseph	2007	Apr 14	E
Roth,	Francis Hyacinth	1985	Dec 30	C
Rothering,	Leo Dominic	2009	Mar 15	C
Rourke,	1. George Justin	1965	Jan 27	E
	2. Gregory Joseph	1943	Sep 27	W
Routh,	Francis Justin	1955	Sep 11	E
Rover,	Thomas Dominic	1998	Apr 7	E
Rubba,	John Camillus	2000	Jun 7	E
Rumaggi,	Robert Louis	1961	Jan 14	E
Rush,	John Dominic	1891	Mar 9	E
Russell,	Joseph Benjamin	2014	Aug 11	C
Rutkauskas,	Benedict Albert	1995	Mar 29	C

Ryan,	1. Bartholomew Edward	1964	Dec 22	C
	2. Francis Aloysius	1897	Oct 5	E
	3. James Raymond	1926	Mar 14	E
	4. John Felix	1964	Jun 18	E
	5. John Joseph	1998	Jul 19	E
	6. John Wilfred	1980	Dec 27	W
	7. Paul Ferrer	1999	Oct 29	C
	8. Thomas Joseph	1877	Nov 25	E
	9. William Bertrand	2004	Jan 10	E
	10. William Regis	1992	Nov 21	E
Sadlier,	Charles Walter	1977	Apr 21	E
Saintourens,	Damien Marie	1920	Sep 26	Nuns (Canada)
Sanchez,	Marian	1945	Jan 10	W (Philippines)
Sandin,	Carl	1916	Feb 20	E
Sanguinetti,	1. Joseph Peter	1997	Jan 23	W
	2. Lawrence Edward	1985	Oct 15	W
Santoro,	1. Charles Henry	2004	Aug 3	C
	2. John	1995	Sep 17	E
Sauro,	Augustine Bonaventure	1956	Jan 30	E
Scallon,	Thomas Augustine	1885	Apr 16	E
Scanlon,	1. George Mark	1937	May 14	E
	2. Paul Edward	2015	Nov 19	W
	3. Paul John Dominic	1996	Dec 21	E
	4. Walter Gabriel	1950	Nov 20	E
Scannell,	Patrick Joseph	1878	Sep 19	E
Schaller,	Harvey Bartholomew	1998	Aug 13	E
Schauer,	Blaise William	1996	Jun 4	W
Scheerer,	1. + Aloysius Louis	1966	Jan 26	E
	2. Berchman Hyacinth	1978	Jan 29	E
Schmidt,	Edward Henry	1985	Oct 3	E
Schneider,	1. Bernard Gabriel	1972	Jul 25	E
	2. Francis Luke	1976	Jan 21	C
	3. Herman Damian	1963	Dec 28	E
	4. John Bernard	1971	Nov 20	C
Schnell,	Leo Walter Edgar	1993	Jan 21	E
Scholz,	Gregory Raphael	1946	Jun 9	C
Schranz,	Ignatius	1959	Apr 10	C
Schratz,	Albert Mark	1996	Oct 23	E (Pakistan)
Schroeder,	Joseph Henry	1942	May 7	C
Schwertner,	Benedict Thomas	1934	Feb 17	E
Schwind,	John Ephrem	1993	Feb 25	C
Scola,	Francis Hugh	1979	Mar 3	E
Scullion,	Matthew Raymond	1991	Feb 17	S
Seamon,	Raymond John	1946	Feb 19	W

Seery,	Franklin Chrysostom	1943	Apr 8	C
Segren,	John Aloysius	1979	Oct 22	E
Serror,	Nicholas Hugh	1972	Nov 27	E
Servente,	Hyacinth Joseph	1958	Jan 21	W
Shaffer,	Bernard Paschal	1965	Sep 24	E
Shanley,	Thomas Quentin	2002	Jan 25	E
Shannon,	1. Charles Thomas	1998	Dec 26	E
	2. Daniel Lambert	1989	Oct 22	E
Sharkey,	Robert Urban	2009	Feb 21	E
Shaw,	1. Richard Raymond Francis	1990	Jun 14	C
	2. Sebastian Henry	1918	Dec 31	W
Shea,	1. Leo Martin	1972	Apr 24	C
	2. Lewis Mary William	2010	Feb 9	C
	3. Thomas Timothy	1980	Sep 15	E
Sheehan,	1. Austin Charles	1968	May 23	E
	2. James Cajetan	1997	Aug 21	E
	3. Joseph Basil	1958	Jan 3	E
	4. Martin Albert	1929	Aug 28	E
	5. Thomas Damian	2000	Jul 24	S
Sheehy,	John Dominic	1873	Oct 17	E
Sheil,	John Aloysius	1941	Jan 7	E
Shepherd,	Patrick	1860	Jun 17	E
Sherer,	Joseph Maurice	1996	Jun 29	E
Sheridan,	1. James Alphonse	1889	Apr 24	E
	2. James Bernard	1998	Jul 20	E
Sherry,	Gilbert Donald	1990	Jun 4	C
Sheuerman,	Joseph Augustine	1862	Apr 2	E
Shields,	Thomas	1878	Apr 30	E
Sibila,	Aloysius Alfred	1975	Apr 6	E
Simones,	Alexis John	1967	Mar 29	C
Simpson,	Vincent Edward	1934	Aug 25	E
Skalko,	Stephen John Dominic	2000	Jul 25	E
Skehan,	1. Paul Augustine	1954	Aug 5	E
	2. Philip Cyprian	1970	Oct 2	E
Skelly,	1. Andrew Patrick	1938	Mar 21	W
	2. Edward Lawrence	1966	May 31	E
Slanina,	Paul Leo	1987	Oct 7	E
Slavin,	Robert Joseph	1961	Apr 24	E
Slinger,	Joseph Henry	1909	Apr 11	E
Sloan,	Andrew James	1984	Nov 26	W
Small,	Mark Paul Francis	1986	Nov 15	E
Smith,	1. Alan Eugene	1985	Jul 29	E
	2. Alphonsus Philip	2007	Nov 4	E
	3. Elwood Ferrer	1992	Jan 9	E

	4. George Innocent	1950	Jun 20	E
	5. Henry Ignatius	1957	Mar 8	E
	6. John Malachy	1963	Sep 24	E
	7. John Reginald	1971	Oct 19	E
	8. Lawrence Ambrose	1945	May 20	E
	9. Mariner Theodore	1971	Mar 10	E
	10. Raymond	1990	Jun 4	E
	11. Stephen Kieran	2018	Apr 4	S
	12. Thomas Bernard	2007	Jan 7	E
	13. Thomas Damian	1988	Apr 7	C
	14. Thomas Joachim	1974	Jul 29	E
Smithers,	Stephen Thomas	2007	Mar 2	S
Snider,	Michael Alexis	1974	Mar 18	E
Snyder,	John Joseph	1987	Mar 12	W
Soeldner,	Joseph Bertrand	1991	Oct 31	E
Spalding,	1. Francis Paul	1959	May 4	E
	2. John Fidelis	1999	Oct 11	E
	3. Martin Pius	1892	Nov 16	E
Sparks,	Howard Timothy	2001	Mar 27	C
Spearing,	James Bernard	1904	Dec 23	E
Spence,	Edward Leo	1949	Jun 25	E
Spencer,	Francis Aloysius	1913	Jun 12	E
Splinter,	Clement Augustine	1923	Feb 21	E
Springman,	Lewis Anthony	1992	Dec 25	E
St. George,	Raymond Bernard	1977	Oct 7	E
Stanley,	Ronald Angelus	2012	Jul 14	E
Stanton,	Joseph Matthew	1950	Mar 14	E
Starrs,	Paul Robert	1984	Jun 3	W
Staszak,	David John	1998	Aug 31	C
Stevenson,	James Raymond	1958	Jan 9	C
Stock,	Michael Edward	1996	May 8	E
Stone,	Richard Aquinas	1976	Feb 9	E
Stratemeier,	George Boniface	1947	Sep 7	E
Strenkert,	Joseph Xavier	1971	Feb 11	E
Suarez-Fernandez,	Eligius	1962	Nov 1	W (Mexico)
Sullivan,	1. James Terence	2001	Jun 28	E
	2. John Alfred	1972	Jul 2	E
	3. John Edward	1981	Mar 26	C
	4. John James	2001	Mar 28	E
	5. John Linus	2011	Dec 2	E
	6. John Pius	1998	Apr 17	E
	7. Joseph John	1960	Jul 18	E
	8. Kenneth Cyprian	1981	Mar 18	E
	9. Robert Patrick	1969	Jul 14	E

	10. Thomas Hyacinth	1966	Jan 29	E
	11. Walter Brendan	1984	Jan 23	E
	12. William Augustine	1935	Mar 22	E
	13. William Dominic	1943	Feb 28	E
Swann,	Denis M.	2005	Aug 26	E
Sweeney,	1. John Michael	1983	Jan 14	E
	2. Paul Luke	1938	Jan 16	E
Tamburello,	John Dominic	2006	Jun 21	S
Tarrier,	William Brendan	2005	Feb 13	E
Taylor,	1. Joseph Bertrand	1979	Dec 11	E
	2. Joseph Celestine	1982	Apr 28	E
Tefft,	William Pius	1991	Feb 17	E
Thamm,	Walter Philip	1941	Dec 7	E
Therres,	Cyril Aloysius	1962	Nov 24	C
Thibault,	Donald Paul	2017	Jan 8	E
Thiel,	James Joachim M.	2004	Oct 6	C
Thissen,	Kevin Cornelius	2005	Jun 2	C
Thomas,	1. Albert Benedict	1989	Nov 19	E
	2. Leo Byron	1997	Nov 18	W
Thornton,	Patrick Luke	1983	Mar 13	E
Thuente,	Theodore Clement Mary	1960	Jul 6	E
Tierney,	1. Arthur Cornelius	1968	Oct 18	E
	2. Walter Jerome	1978	Jul 24	E
Timony,	James Clement	1930	Jan 9	E
Timpane,	Thomas Dominic	1929	Mar 21	E
Towle,	Daniel Raymond	1936	Feb 27	E
Townsend,	1. Anselm M. Thomas	1977	Oct 30	C
	2. Ralph Valerian	2011	Mar 6	E
Traynor,	John Charles	1879	Apr 15	W
Treacy,	Jerome Timothy	1973	Nov 2	C
Trutter,	Richard Simon	2000	Feb 5	C
Tucker,	Robert Ignatius	1971	Dec 18	C
Tuite,	William Raymond	1833	May 25	E
Tully,	Thomas	1901	Dec 4	E
Turbitt,	Robert Gabriel	1924	Aug 18	E
Turner,	Jeremiah Pius	1892	Oct 6	E
Turon,	Louis Luke	2013	Nov 24	E
Turzick,	John Alphonsus	1979	Apr 22	E
Twohig,	Francis John	1945	Jun 16	E
Tyulen,	Clement Daniel	2014	Apr 10	Nigeria
Up de Graff,	William Linus	1985	Jun 7	S
Urbanc,	Mannes	1965	Dec 4	C
Urquhart,	John Dominic	1856-57	Dec ?	E
Vahey,	Richard Edward	1987	Apr 12	E

Valine,	Hyacinth Joseph	1992	Sep 26	W
Vallely,	John Philip	1930	Nov 6	E
Van Becelaere,	Edward Lawrence	1946	Apr 12	C
Van den Broek,	John Theodore	1851	Nov 5	E (Germany)
Van den Wildenberg,	Henry John Dominic	1921	Apr 24	E
Van Erkel,	Adolph Isnard	1990	Oct 12	E (Flanders)
van Rooy,	Daniel Walter	1985	Nov 10	C
Van To Mai,	Peter	2008	Apr 10	S
Vander Heyden,	Lawrence Francis	1960	Mar 19	C
Vann,	Gerald Lawrence	1963	Jul 14	W (England)
Vargas Soleto,	Walter	2003	Dec 8	C (Bolivia)
Vaughn,	Robert William	2016	Dec 19	E
Vázquez Pavón,	José Leonardo	1997	Oct 14	S
Velez,	Felix	1943	Jul 23	W (Spain)
Verschure,	Mark Charles	1956	Oct 9	C
Vicente,	1. Francisco V.	2017	Jun 17	W
	2. Isidore V.	2017	May 22	S
Vilarassa,	Sadoc Francis	1888	Mar 17	W
Vinyes,	Vincent Francis	1892	Jul 2	W
Vishigh,	Igba Rumen	2000	Jan 17	N (Nigeria)
Vitie,	Edward Anselm	1980	Feb 9	E
Vivier,	Joseph Raymond	1958	Apr 11	E
Vizcarra,	Angel	2004	Dec 5	S
Vollmer,	Rudolph Francis	1971	Nov 6	E
Wade,	Harold Adrian	1989	Jun 4	E
Waldron,	Martin Augustine	1926	Dec 9	E
Walker,	1. Augustine Peter	1900	Jun 22	E
	2. James Bernard	1984	Jul 5	C
	3. Richard Vernon	1944	Nov 18	E
	4. Robert Linus	2016	Jan 4	E
Wall,	Kevin Albert	1988	Nov 14	W
Wallace,	William Augustine	2015	Mar 4	E
Walsh,	1. Augustine Ignatius	1908	Jul 19	E
	2. Francis Joseph	1961	Jul 19	W
	3. Jerome Matthias	2013	Nov 3	C
	4. Joachim John	1962	Mar 8	E
	5. John Bernard	1968	Oct 19	E
	6. John Dominic	1982	May 8	E
	7. John Nicholas	1982	Dec 21	S
	8. Joseph Alphonsus	1963	Jan 9	E
	9. Paul Patrick	2003	Jan 22	E
	10. William Antoninus	1981	Apr 30	E
Walter,	Gordon Frederick	1976	Jan 10	C
Ward,	1. Daniel John	1966	Nov 15	W

	2. Hubert Francis	1983	Jun 6	W
Warnock,	John Jordan	1955	Oct 27	E
Warren,	Constantius Edward	1923	Jul 27	W
Waskowski,	Bernard Giles	1970	Jan 22	C
Watson,	James Vincent	2010	Oct 16	E
Way,	Edmund John	2008	Nov 22	E
Weber,	1. Lucius M.	1989	Apr 24	S
	2. Richard Vincent	1996	Jan 7	C
Weiland,	Thomas Luke	1960	May 28	E
Weisheipl,	James Athansius	1984	Dec 30	C
Welch,	Sadoc Francis	1912	Oct 13	W
Welsh,	1. Charles Pius	1941	Feb 2	E
	2. Hubert Hugo	1954	Jan 14	E
	3. Joseph John	1948	Sep 18	E
	4. Martin Stanislaus	1961	Jun 21	E
Wendell,	Francis Norbert	1970	May 9	E
Werner,	Bernard Constantius	1985	Sep 15	E
Wessels,	John Cletus	2009	Aug 12	C
West,	Peter James	1979	Dec 18	C
Whalen,	1. Vincent Regis	1952	Sep 8	C
	2. William Leo	1957	Oct 8	E
Whelan,	1. Andrew Michael	1953	Oct 25	E
	2. + James	1878	Feb 18	E
	3. Michael	1884	Sep 30	E
White,	1. Antoninus John	1893	Mar 4	W
	2. Victor Gordon	1960	May 22	W (England)
Whittaker,	John Fabian	1997	Apr 2	E
Wilburn,	James Stanislaus	1927	Feb 5	E
Wild,	Henry Vincent	1959	Oct 6	E
Wilks,	Bede Francis Eugene	2011	Nov 25	W
Willet,	William Thomas	1824	May 6	E
Williams,	John Victor	1963	Aug 28	E
Willoughby,	Malcom Sylvester	2015	Nov 19	E
Wilson,	1. Ambrose Francis	1911	Oct 18	W
	2. Charles Pius	1992	Feb 15	E
	3. Eugene Aloysius	1939	Nov 27	E
	4. George Augustine Joseph	1884	Feb 20	E
	5. Samuel Thomas	1824	May 23	E
Windbacher,	Peter Ambrose	2001	Oct 8	N (Nigeria-C)
Winters,	Andrew James	1980	Apr 10	S
Wreisner,	Richard Hugh	2001	Sep 8	C
Wrinn,	James Timothy	2006	Aug 9	S
Wrobleski,	Victor Humbert	1973	Jan 28	C
Wynn,	Daniel Antoninus	1949	May 27	C

Wyss,	Joseph Melchior	1994	Jan 19	S
Yonkus,	Francis Emmanuel	1980	Apr 20	E
Young,	1. Nicholas Dominic	1878	Nov 28	E
	2. Nicholas Raymond	1876	Jul 24	E
	3. Robert	1812	Dec ?	E
Zagar,	John Janko	2013	May 1	W
Zammit,	Paul Natale	1995	Sep 21	W
Zarlenga,	1. Rinaldo Angelico	1986	Feb 28	C (Rome)
	2. Vincent Italo	2010	Jun 13	C (Rome)
Zelaya Sanchez,	Eduardo Ponciano	1976	Dec 14	C (Boliva)
Ziuraitis,	Vitoldus Thomas	1990	Apr 15	E
Zusy,	1. James Bonaventure	2004	Jul 3	C
	2. Robert Dennis	2000	Aug 6	C
Zvirblis,	Bruno Casimir	1972	Nov 9	E

Made in the USA
Middletown, DE
14 November 2018